imagimorphia

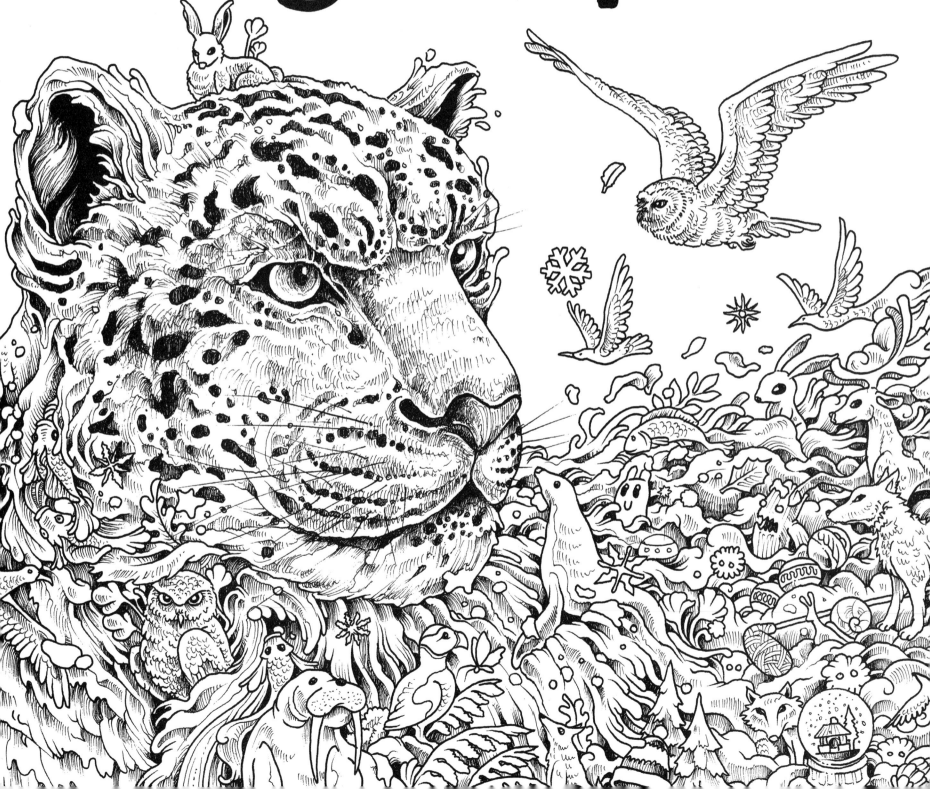

P9-CQR-523

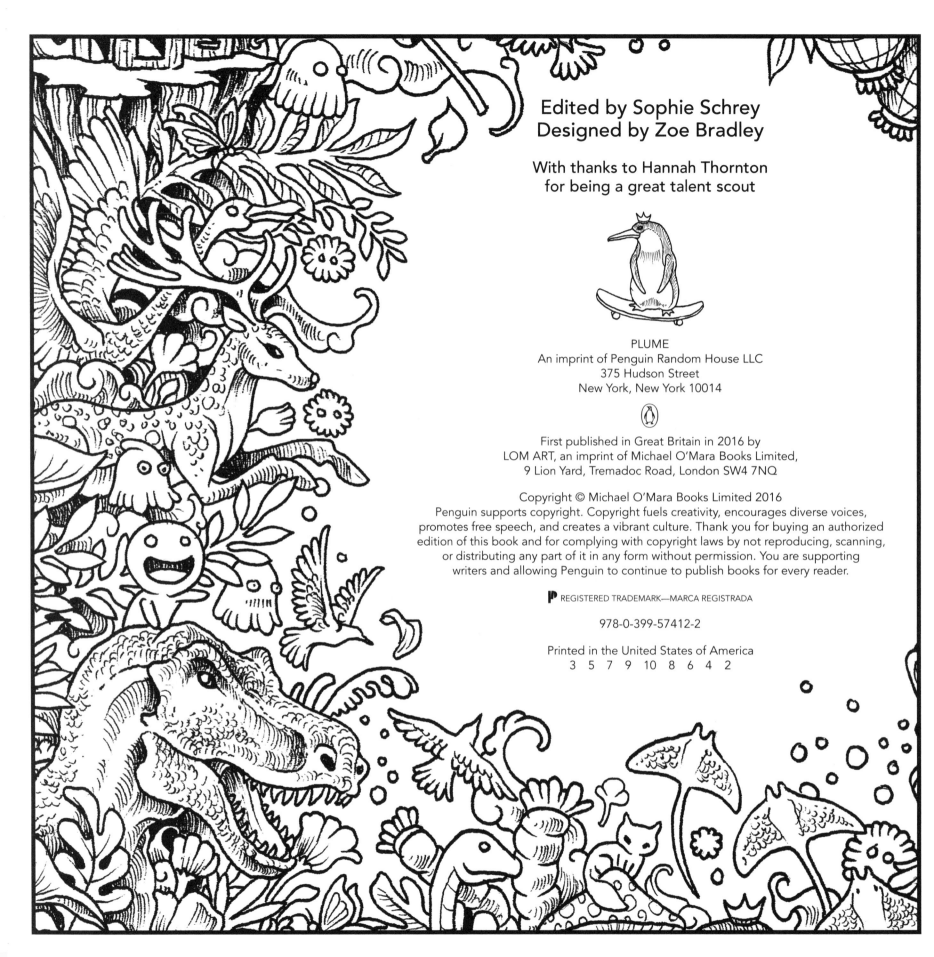

Edited by Sophie Schrey
Designed by Zoe Bradley

With thanks to Hannah Thornton
for being a great talent scout

PLUME
An imprint of Penguin Random House LLC
375 Hudson Street
New York, New York 10014

First published in Great Britain in 2016 by
LOM ART, an imprint of Michael O'Mara Books Limited,
9 Lion Yard, Tremadoc Road, London SW4 7NQ

Copyright © Michael O'Mara Books Limited 2016
Penguin supports copyright. Copyright fuels creativity, encourages diverse voices,
promotes free speech, and creates a vibrant culture. Thank you for buying an authorized
edition of this book and for complying with copyright laws by not reproducing, scanning,
or distributing any part of it in any form without permission. You are supporting
writers and allowing Penguin to continue to publish books for every reader.

REGISTERED TRADEMARK—MARCA REGISTRADA

978-0-399-57412-2

Printed in the United States of America
3   5   7   9   10   8   6   4   2

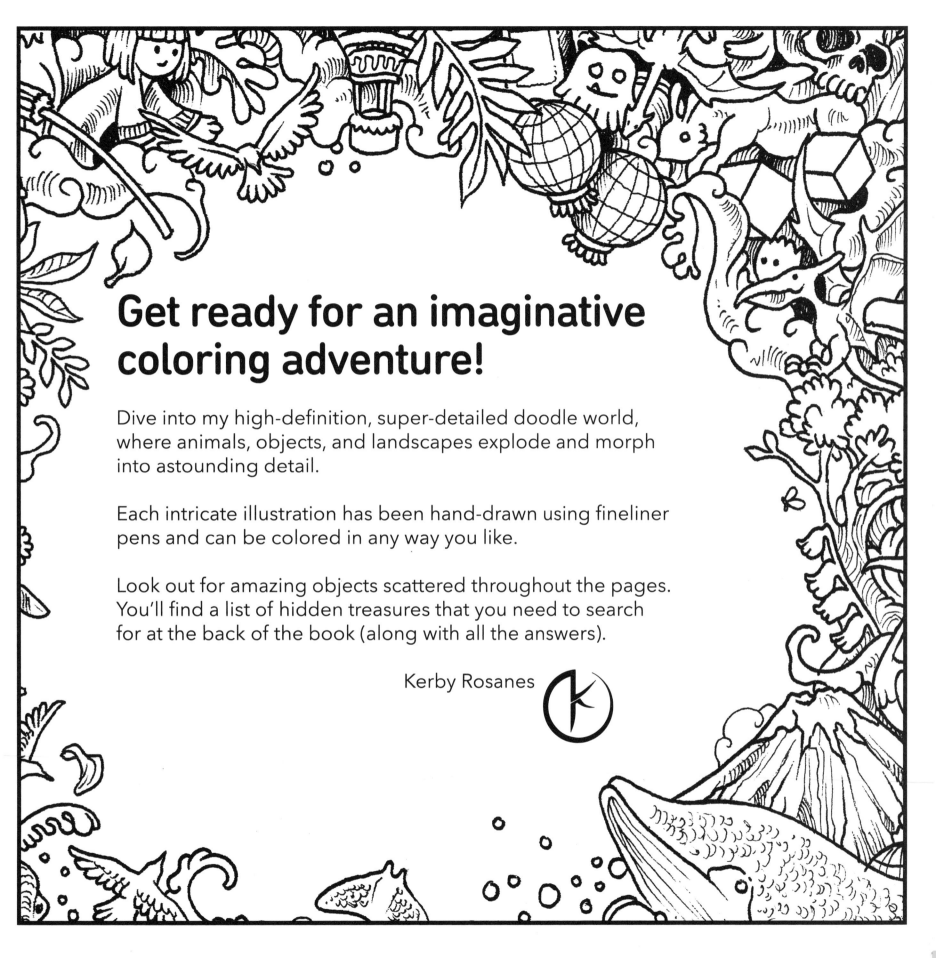

Get ready for an imaginative coloring adventure!

Dive into my high-definition, super-detailed doodle world, where animals, objects, and landscapes explode and morph into astounding detail.

Each intricate illustration has been hand-drawn using fineliner pens and can be colored in any way you like.

Look out for amazing objects scattered throughout the pages. You'll find a list of hidden treasures that you need to search for at the back of the book (along with all the answers).

Kerby Rosanes

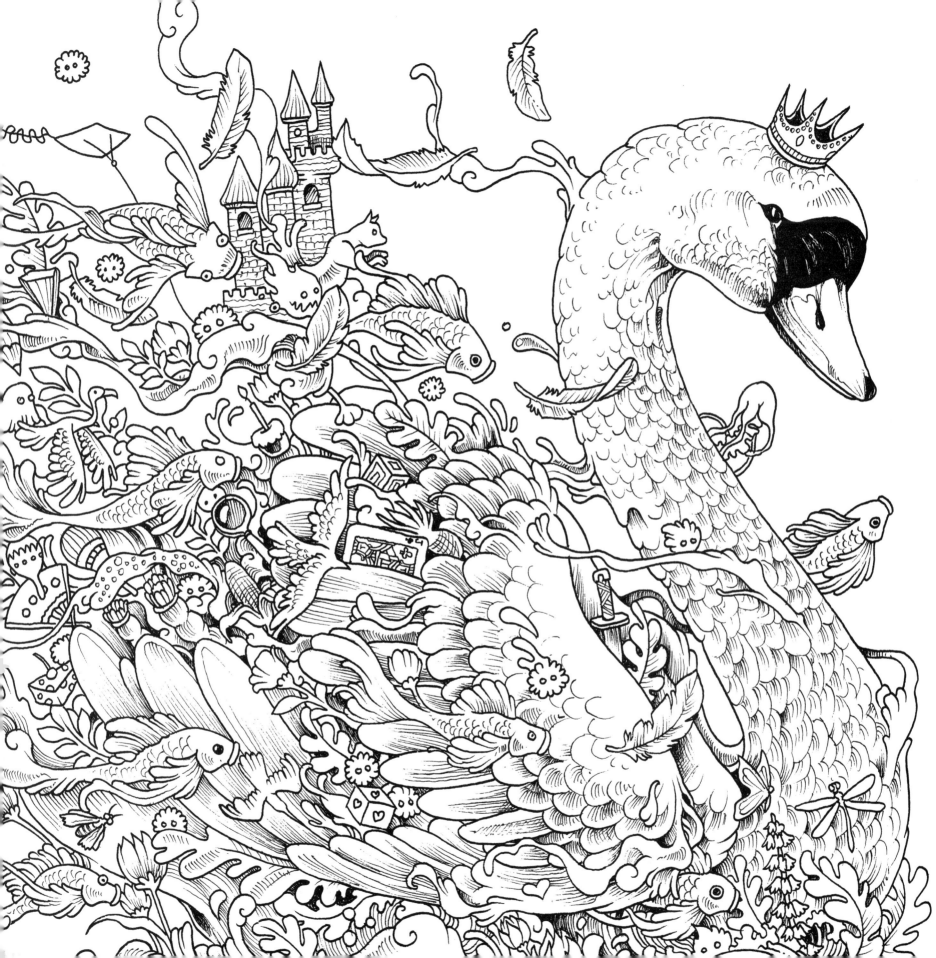

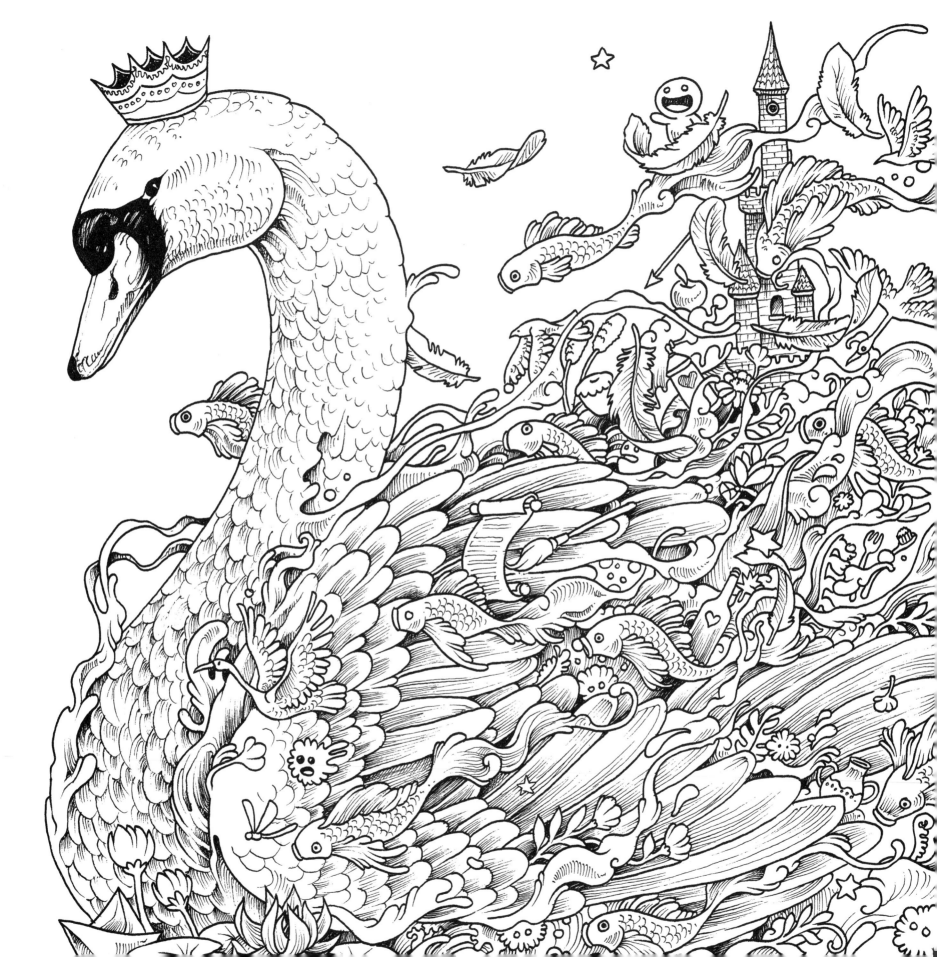

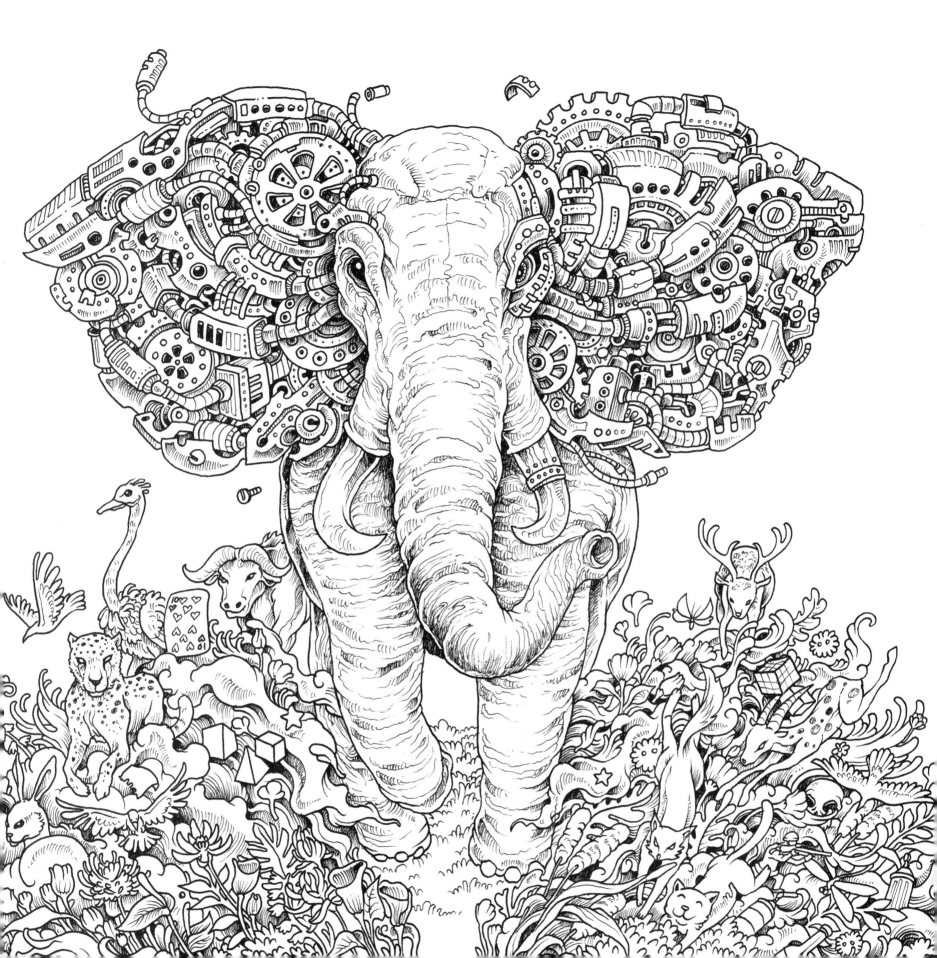

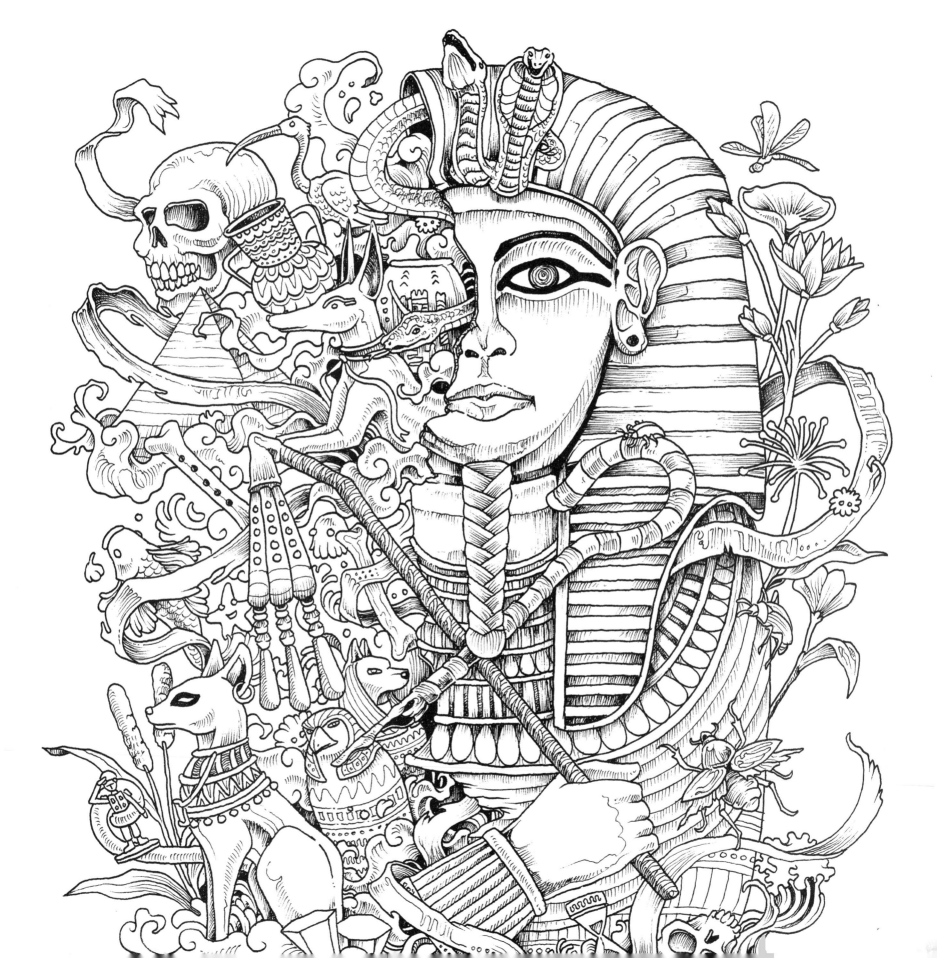

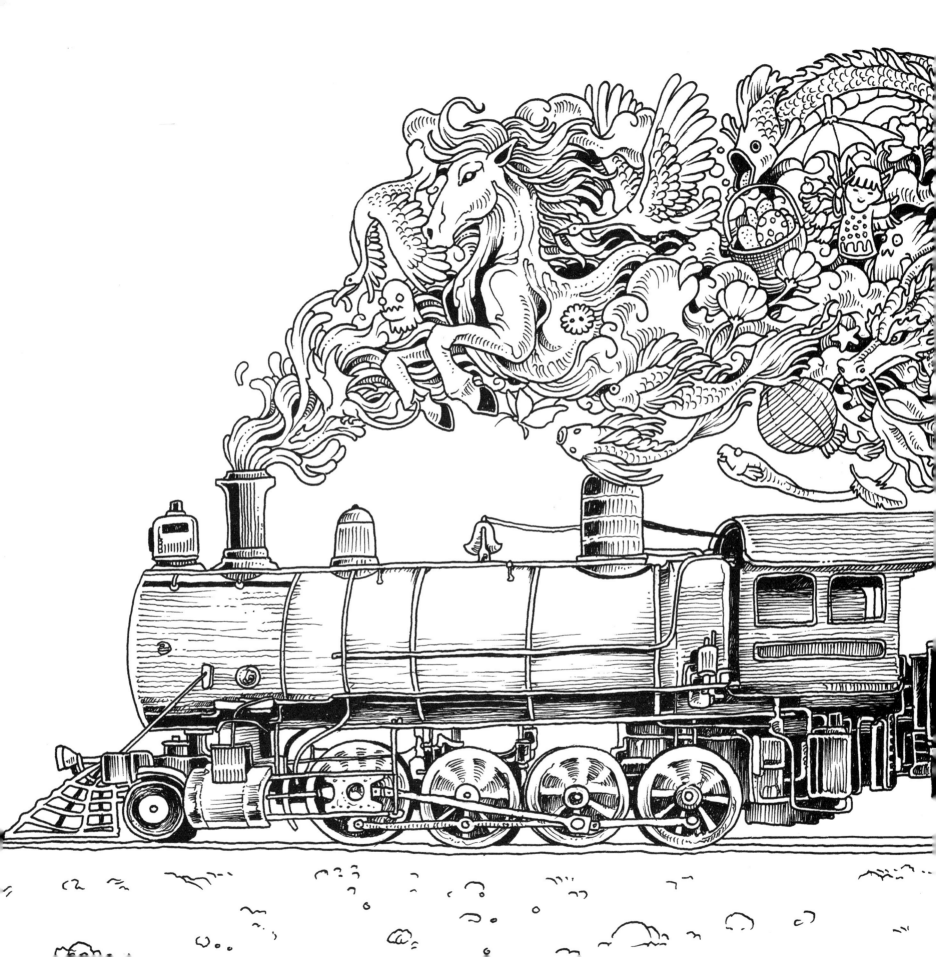

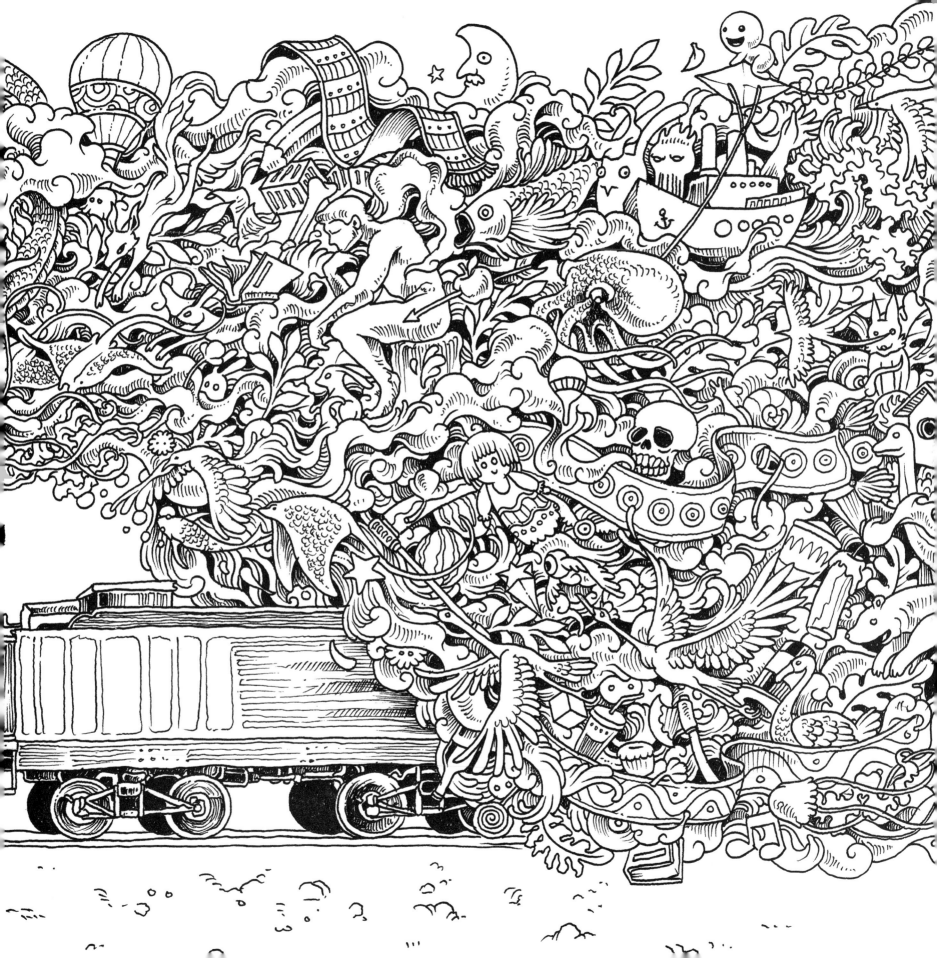

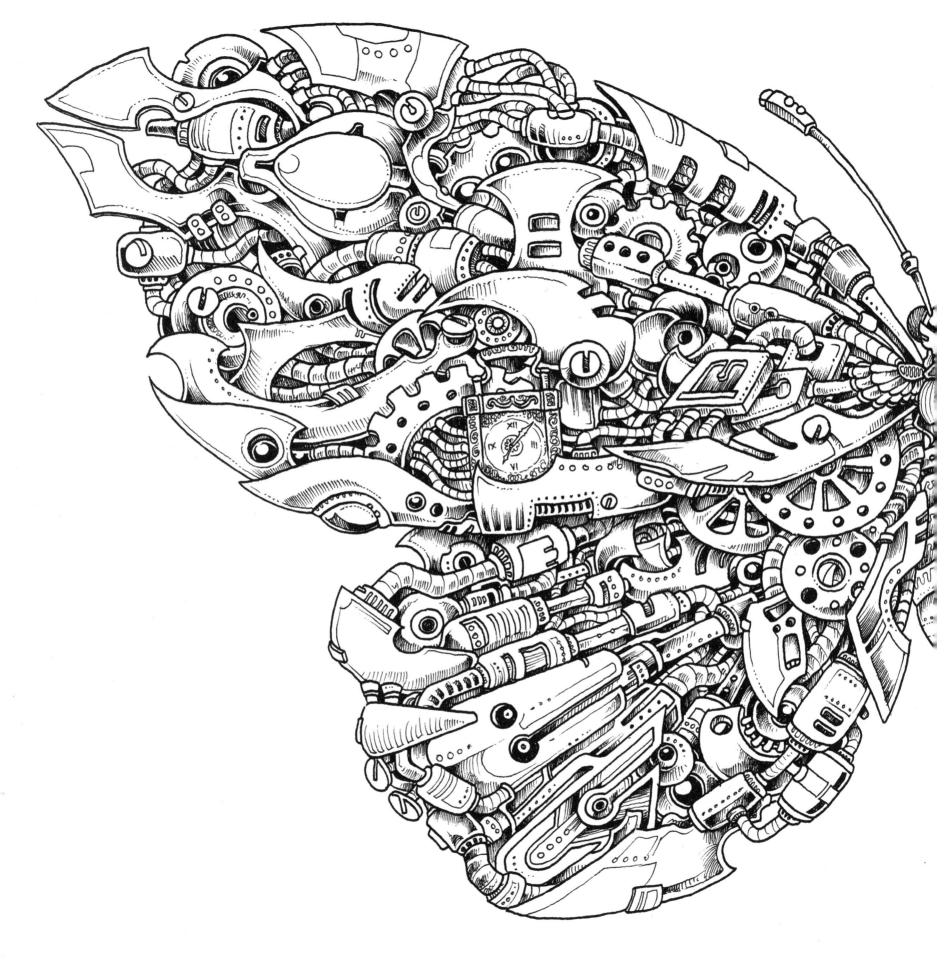

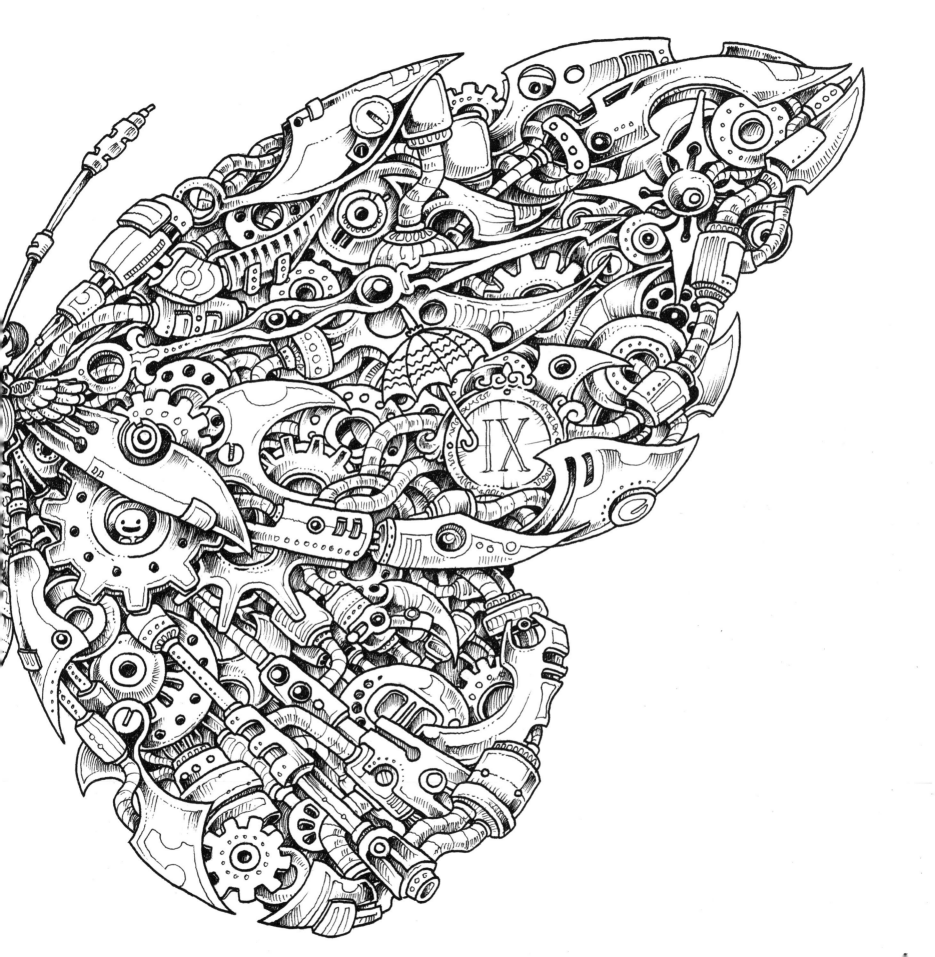

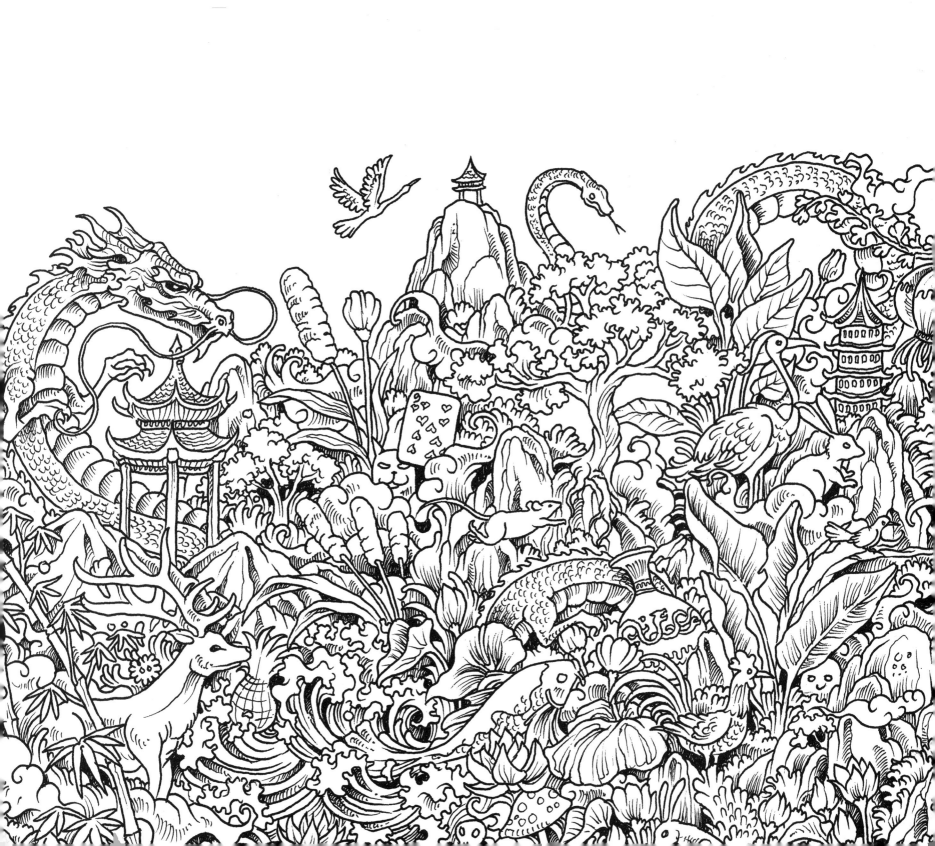

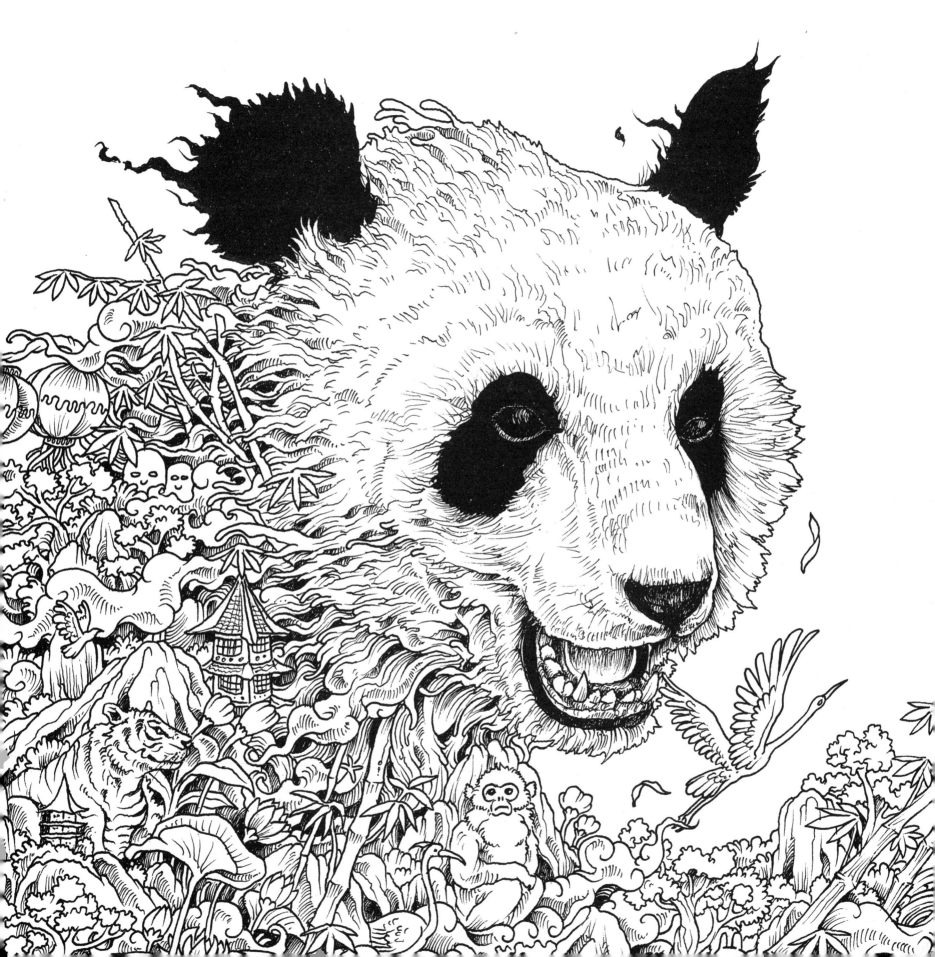

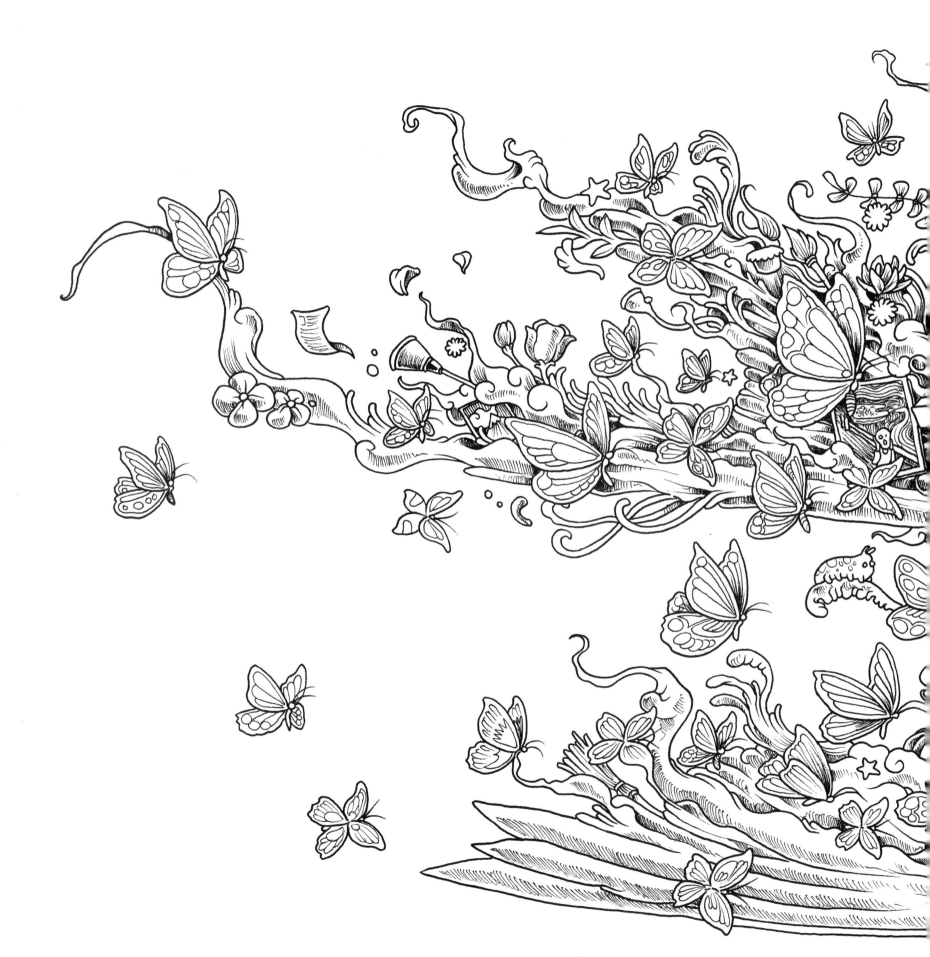

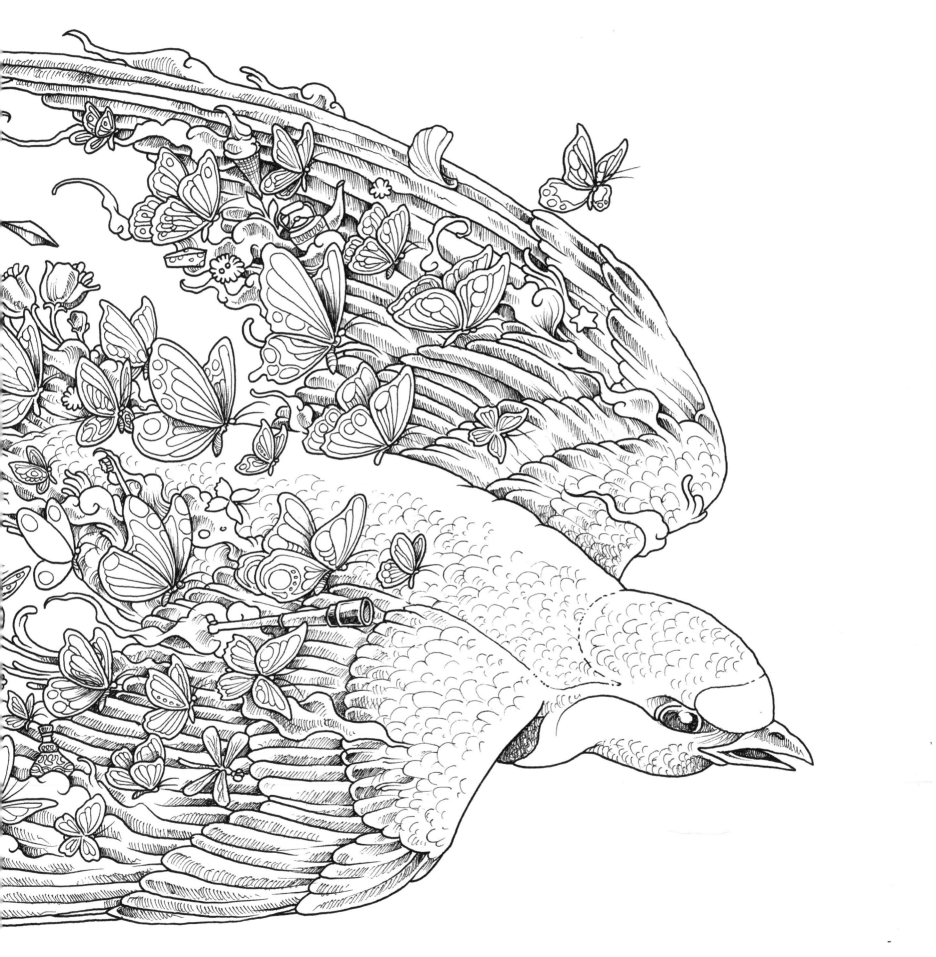

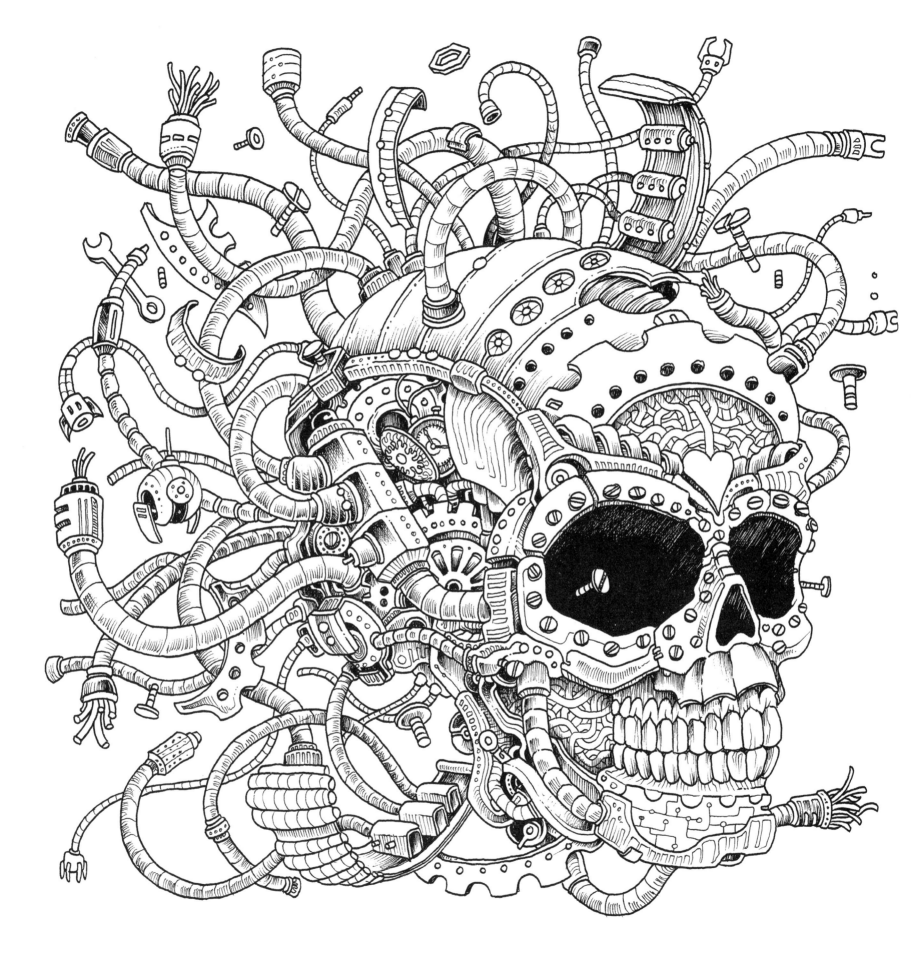

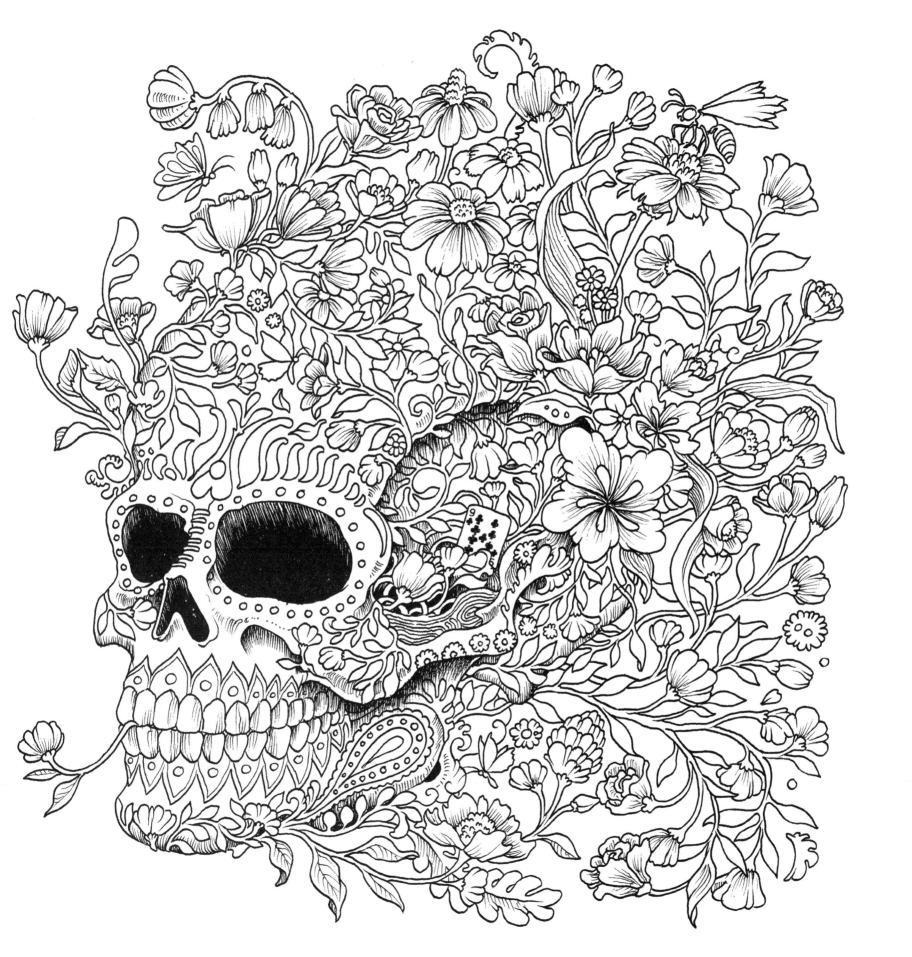

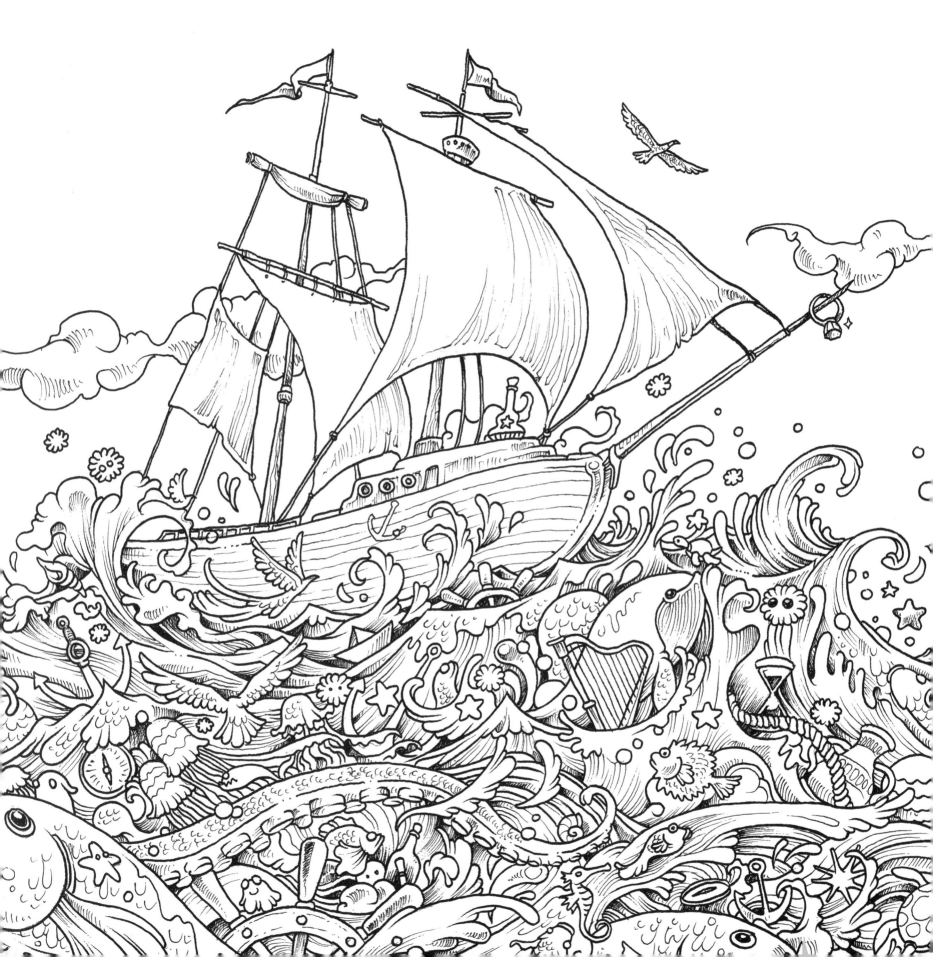

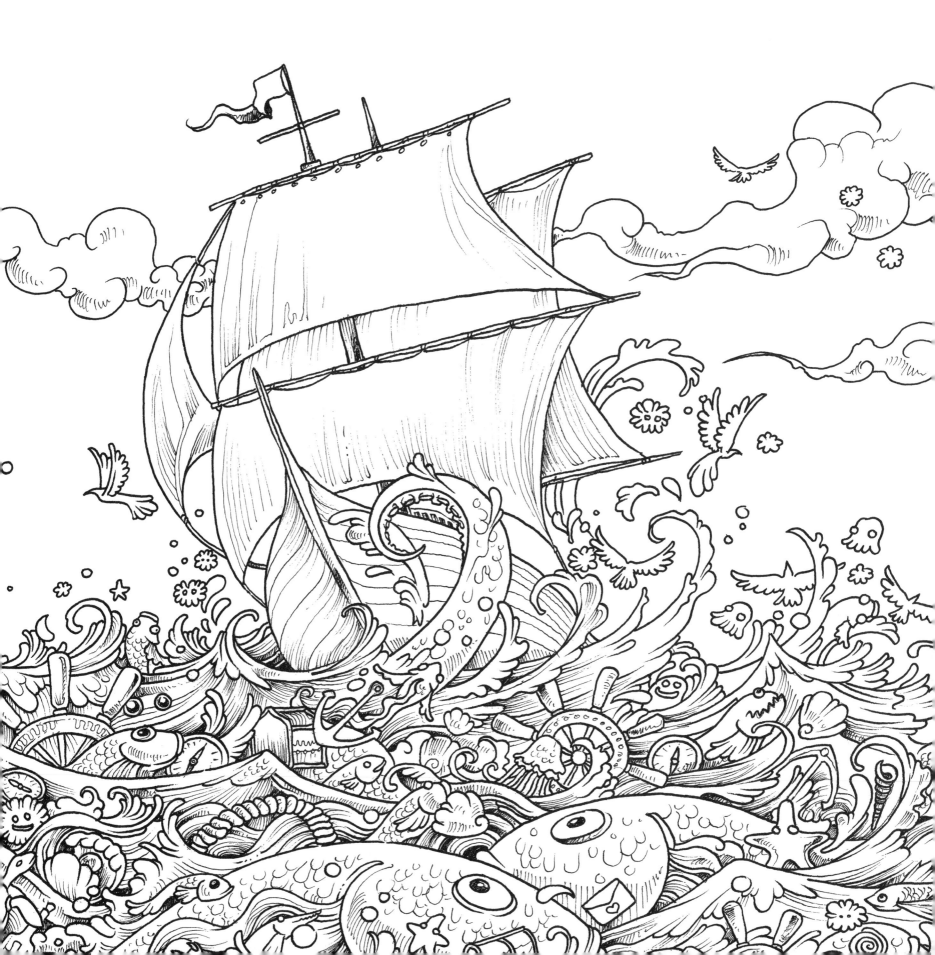

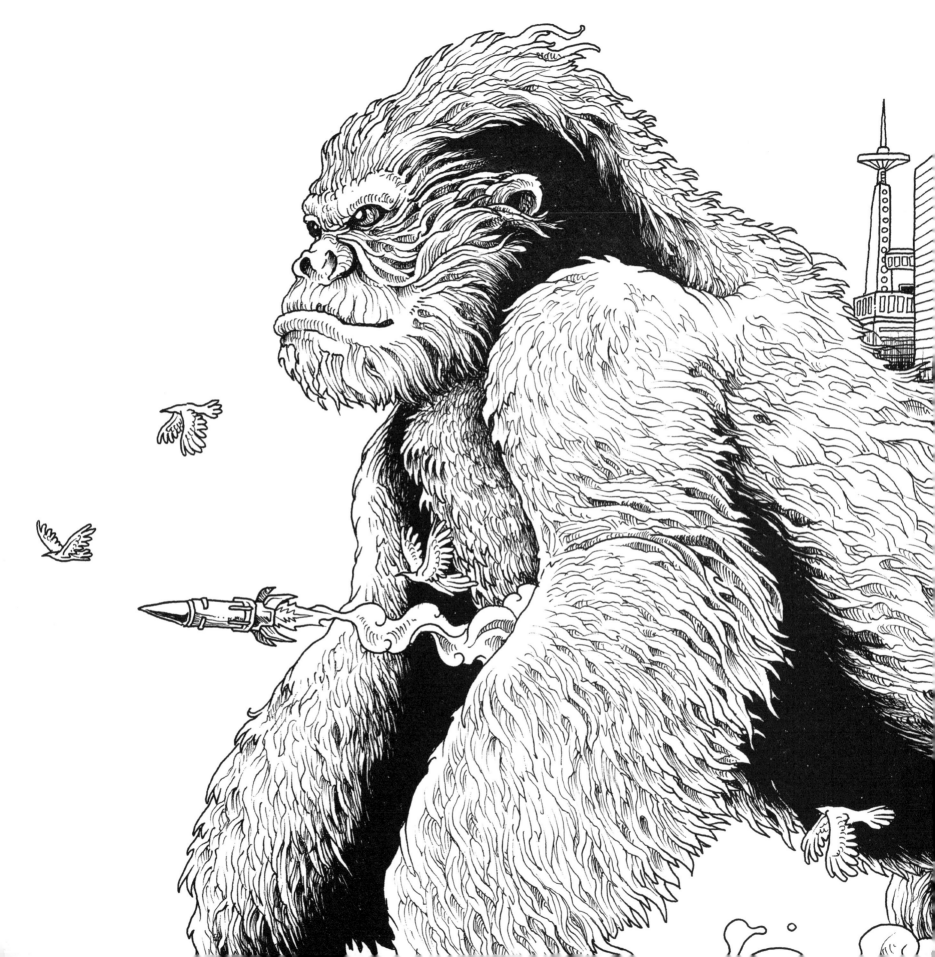

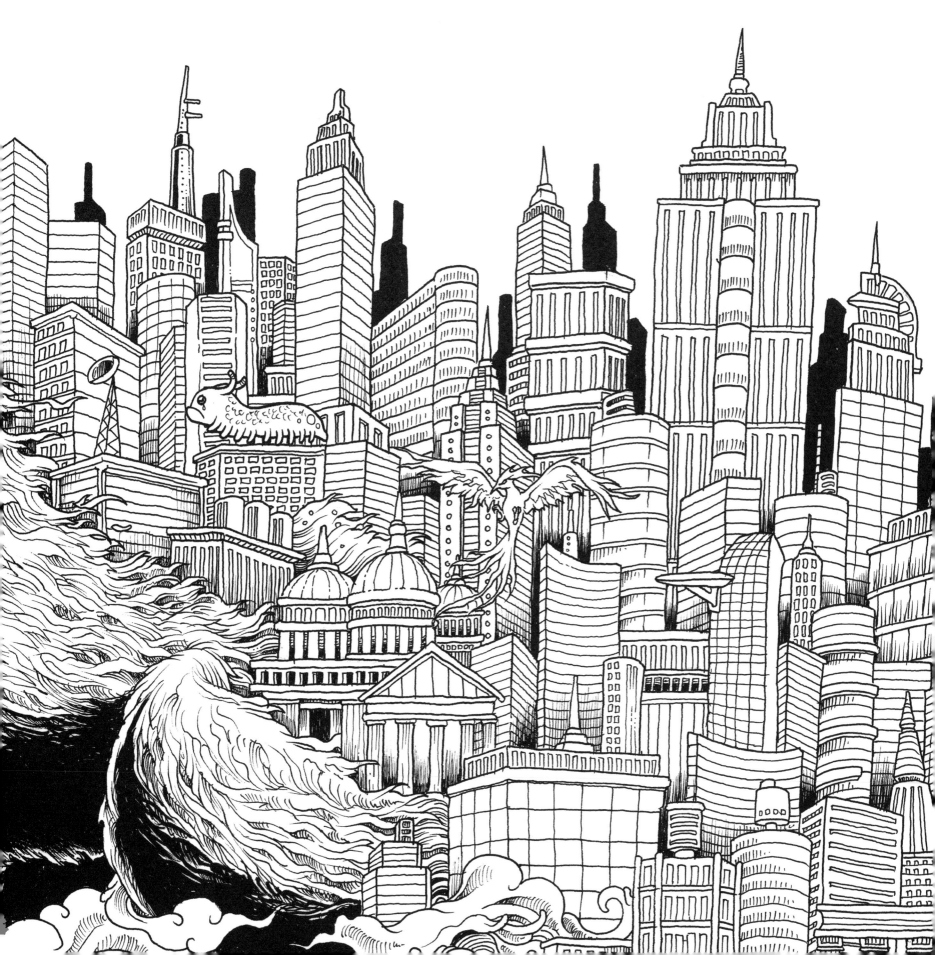

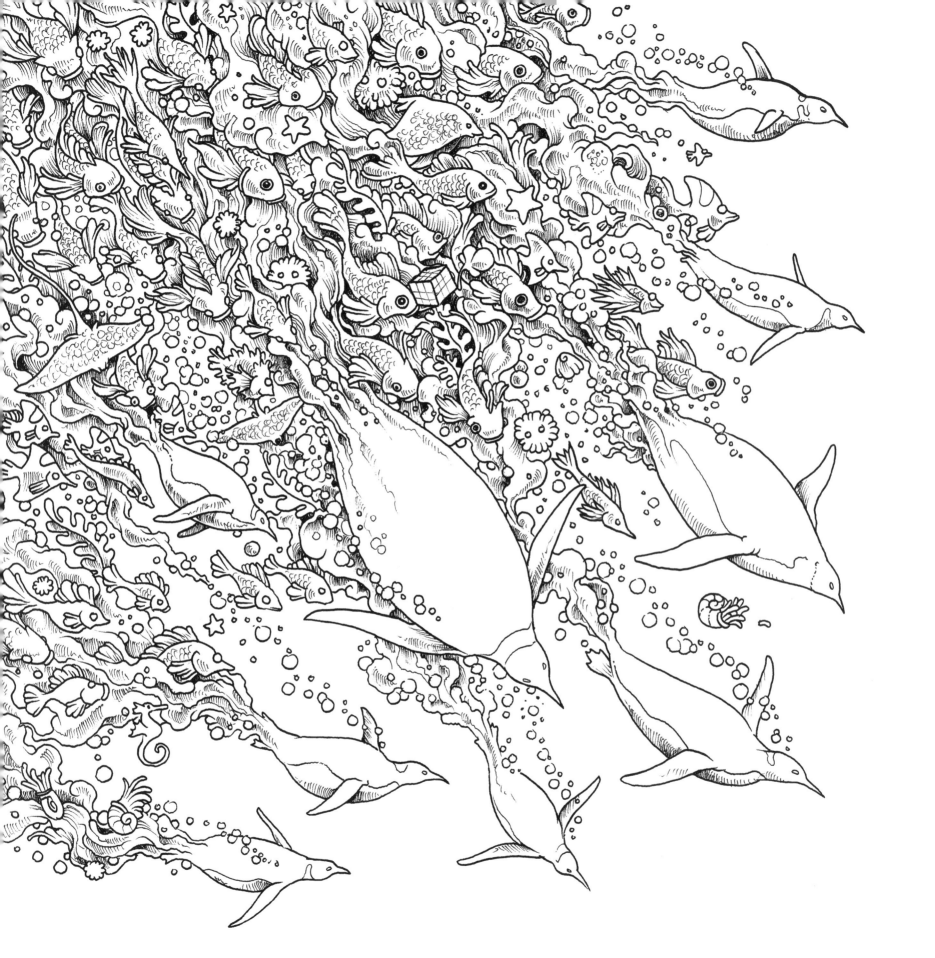

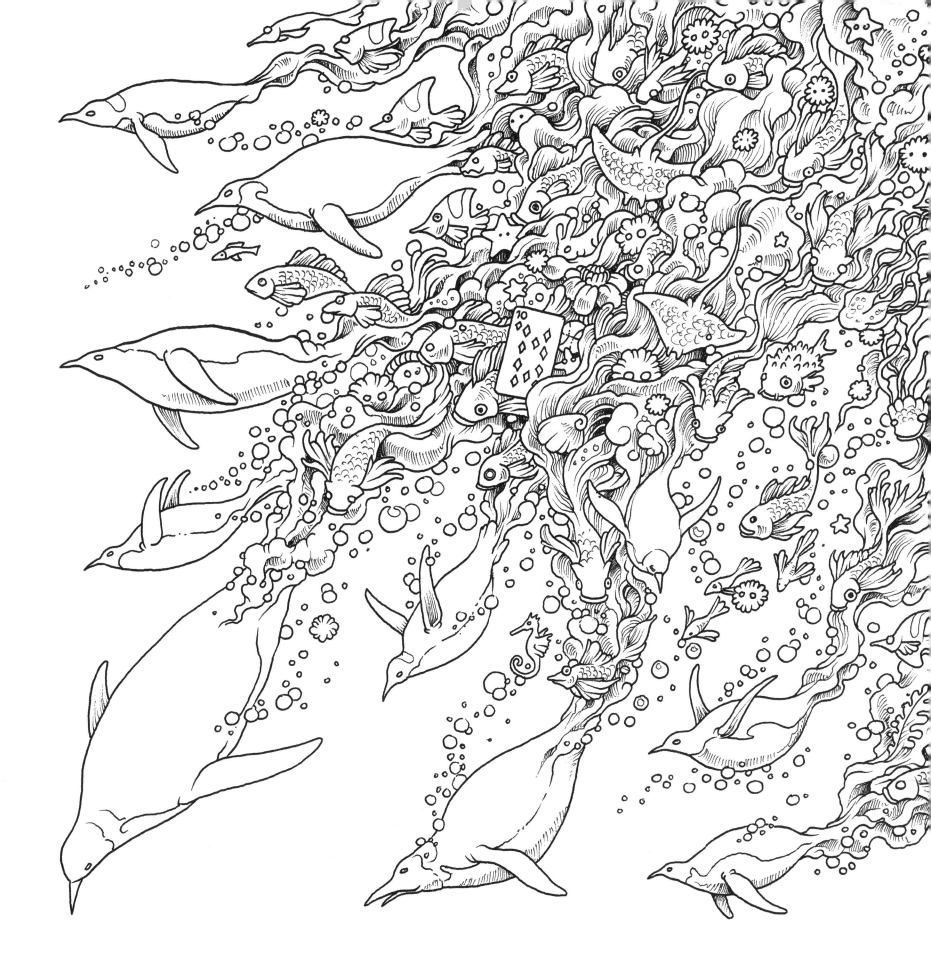

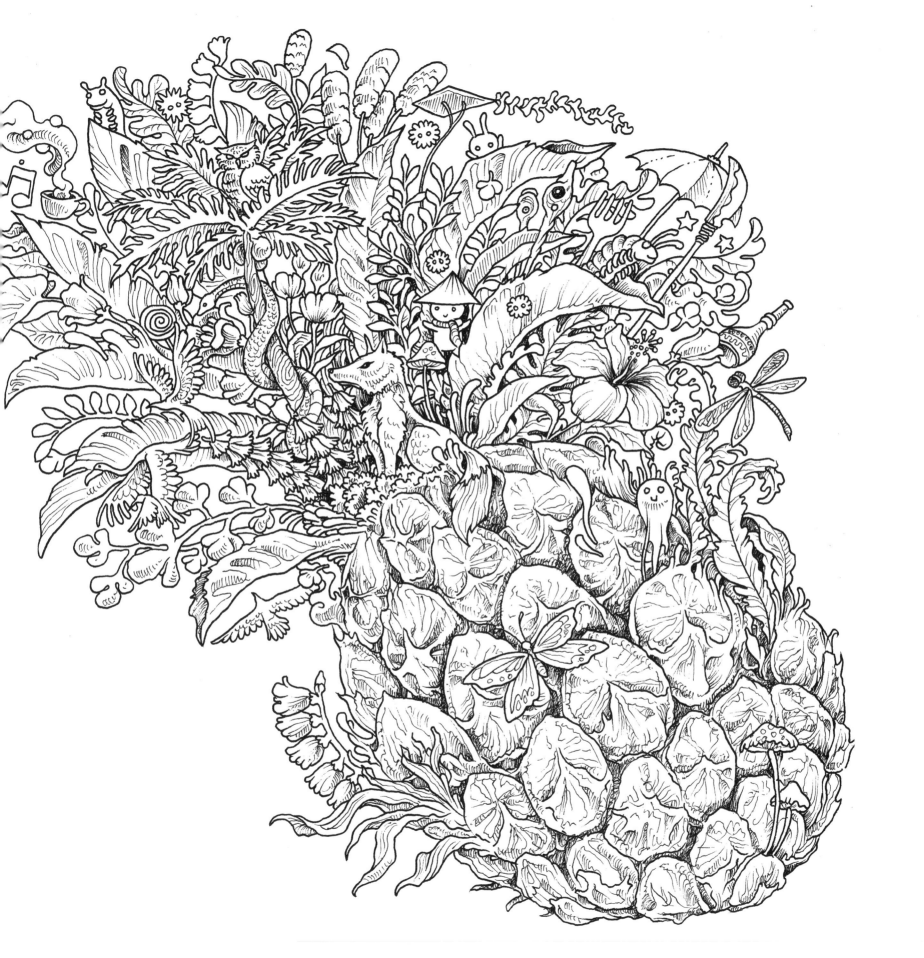

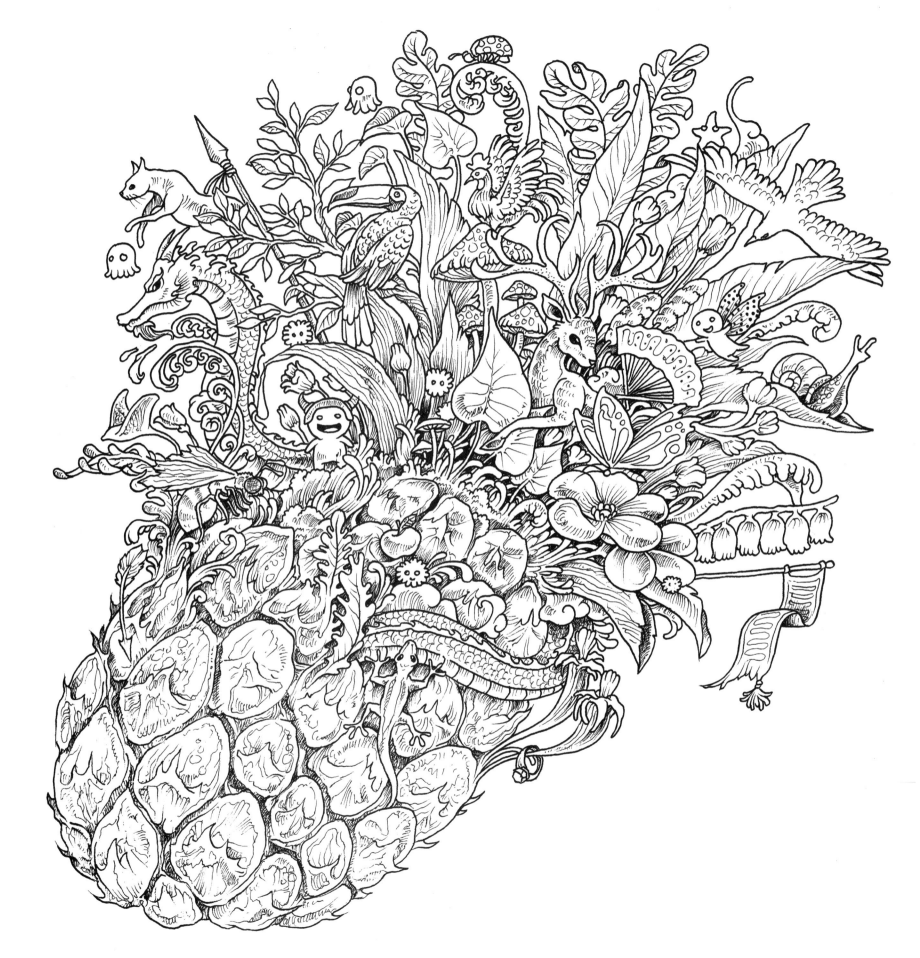

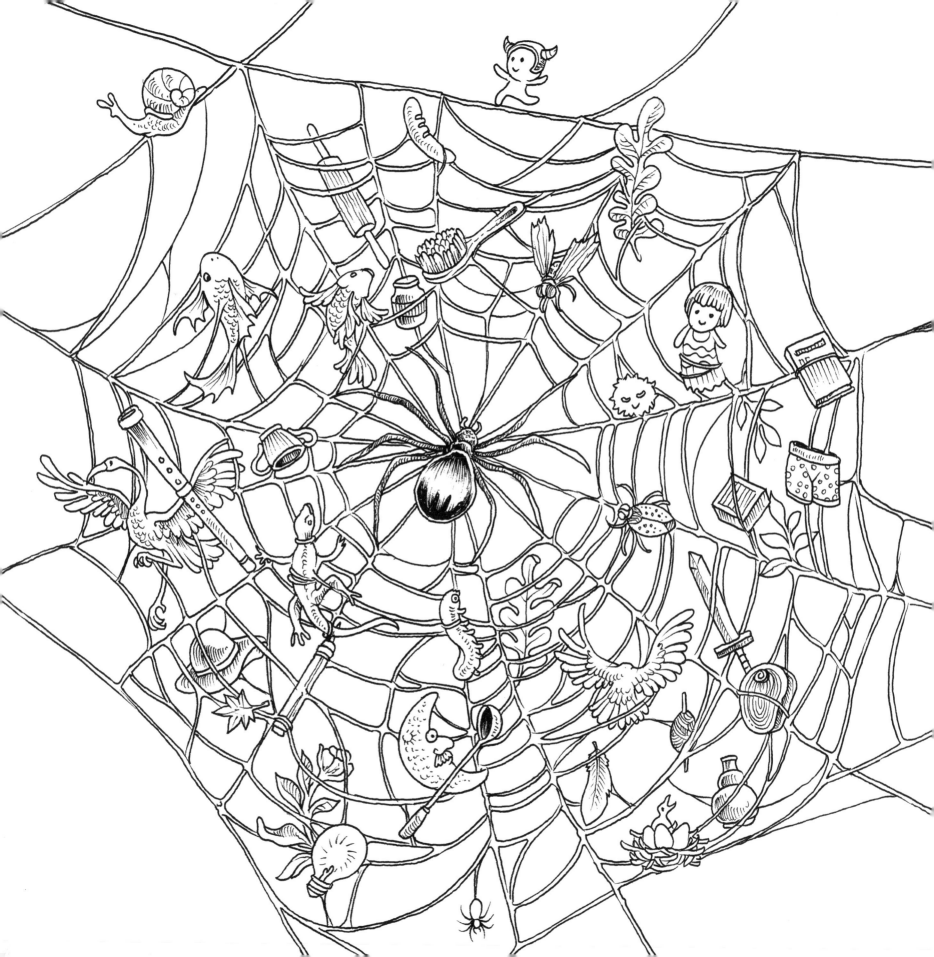

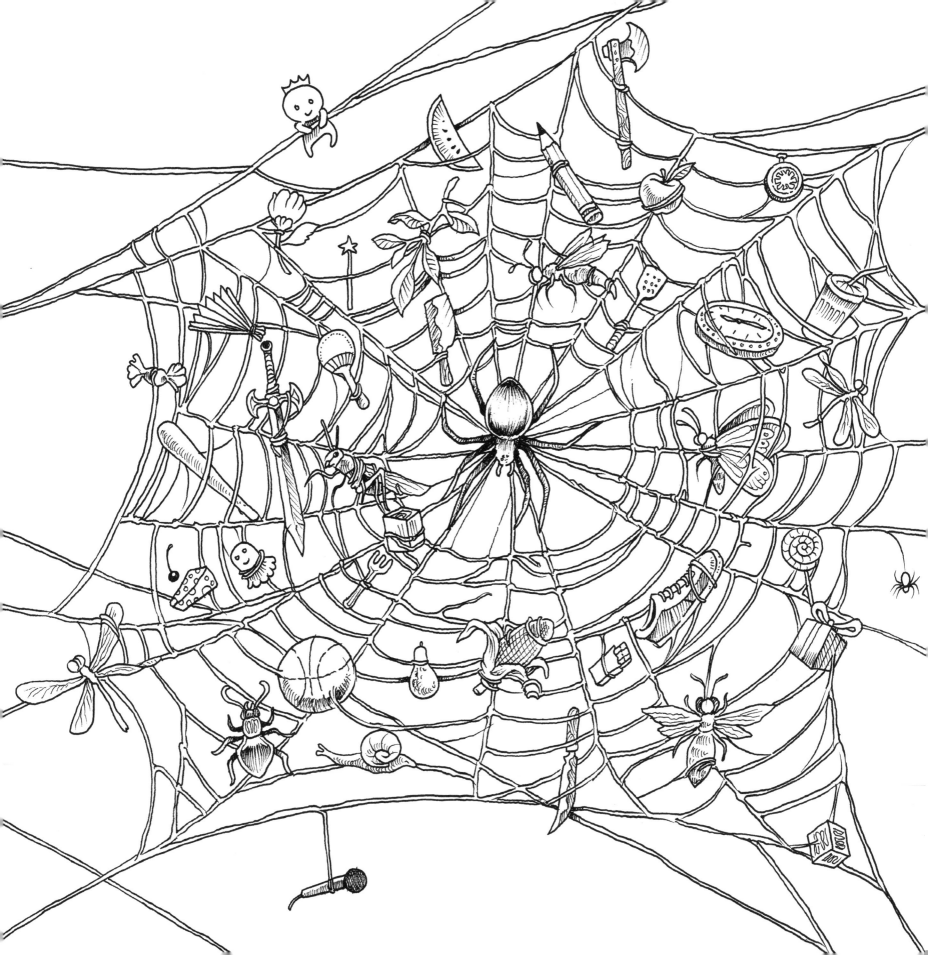

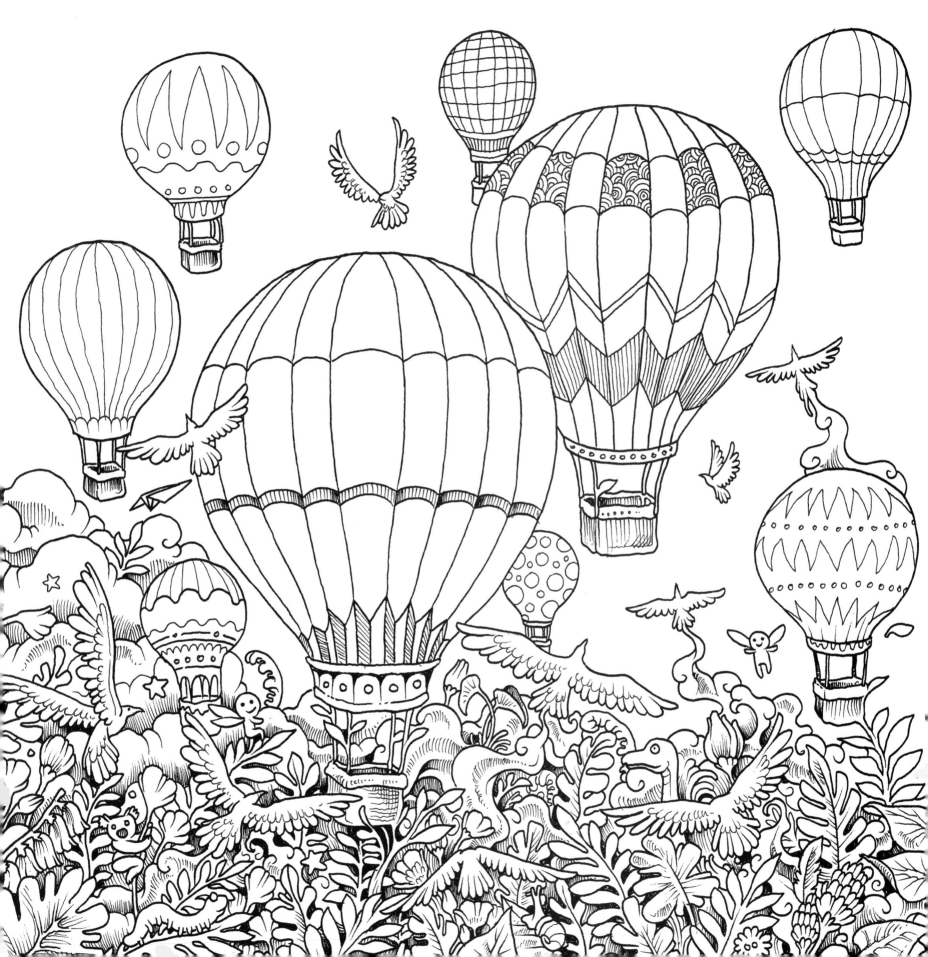

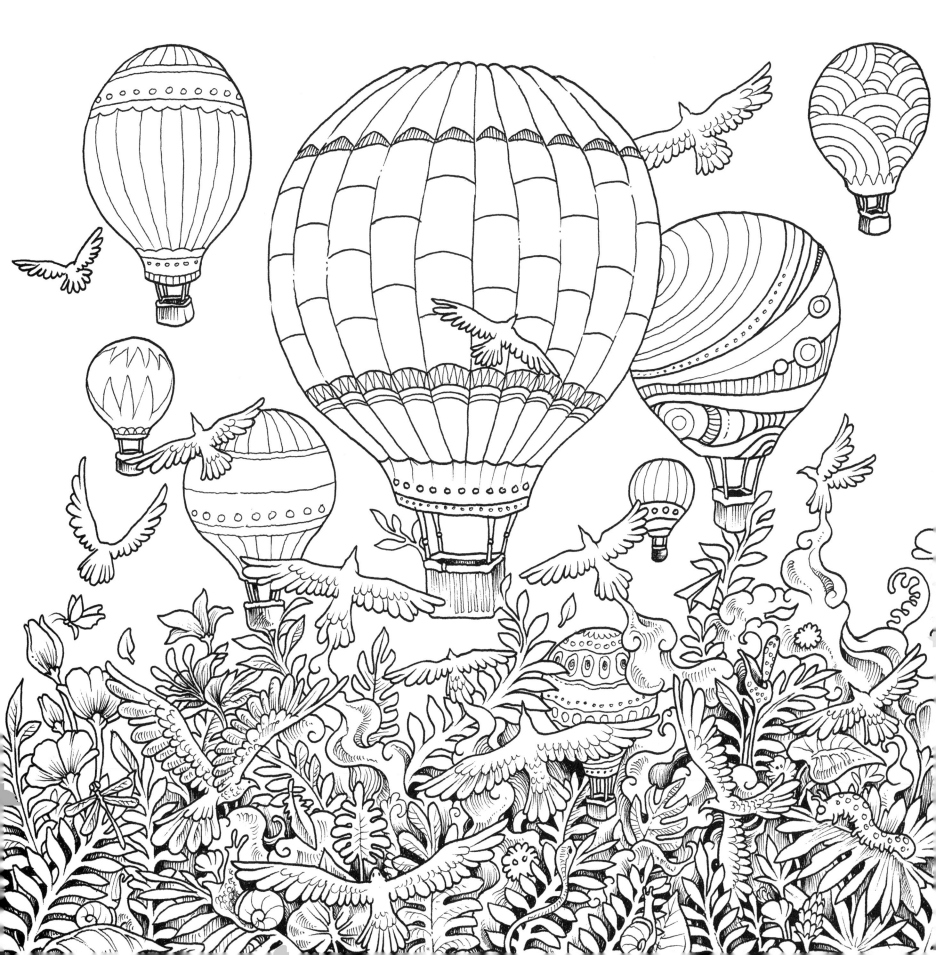

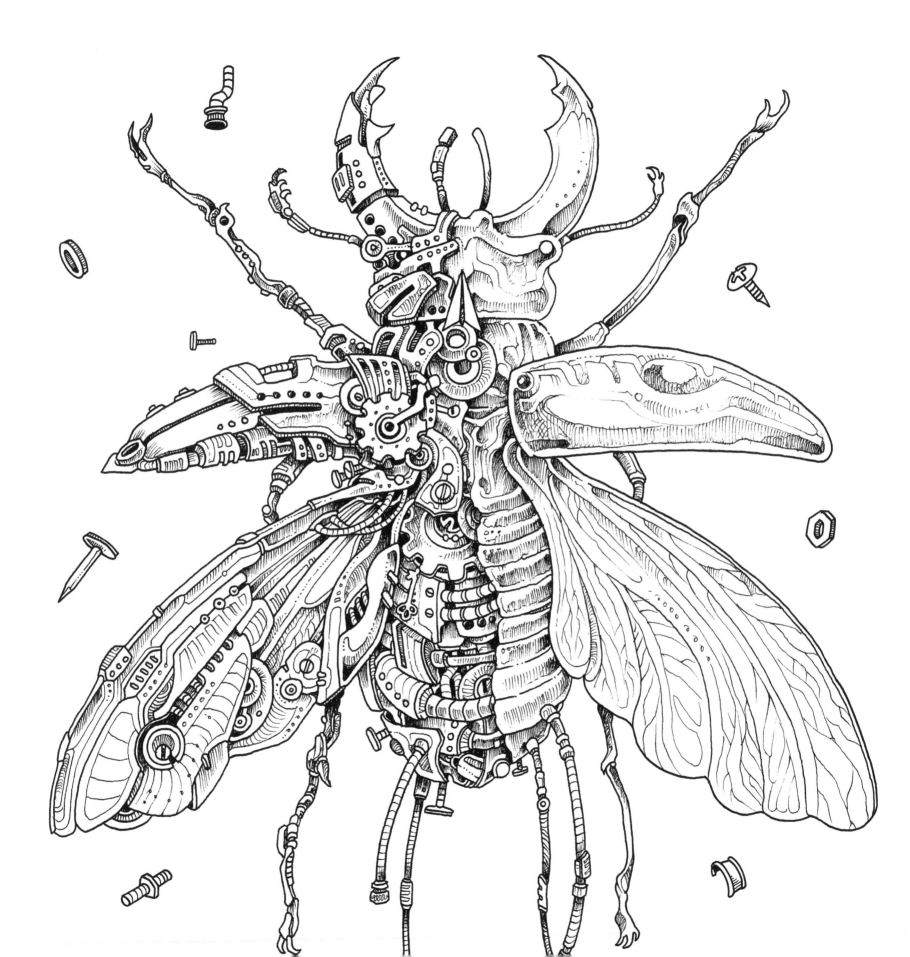

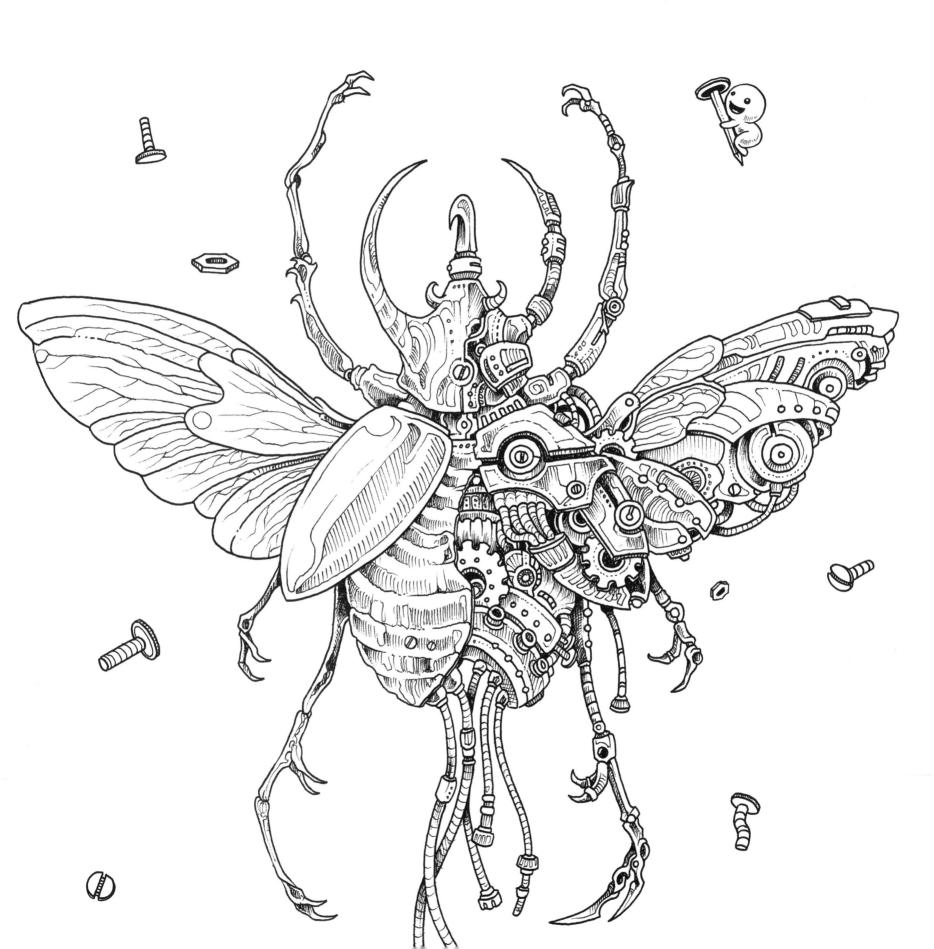

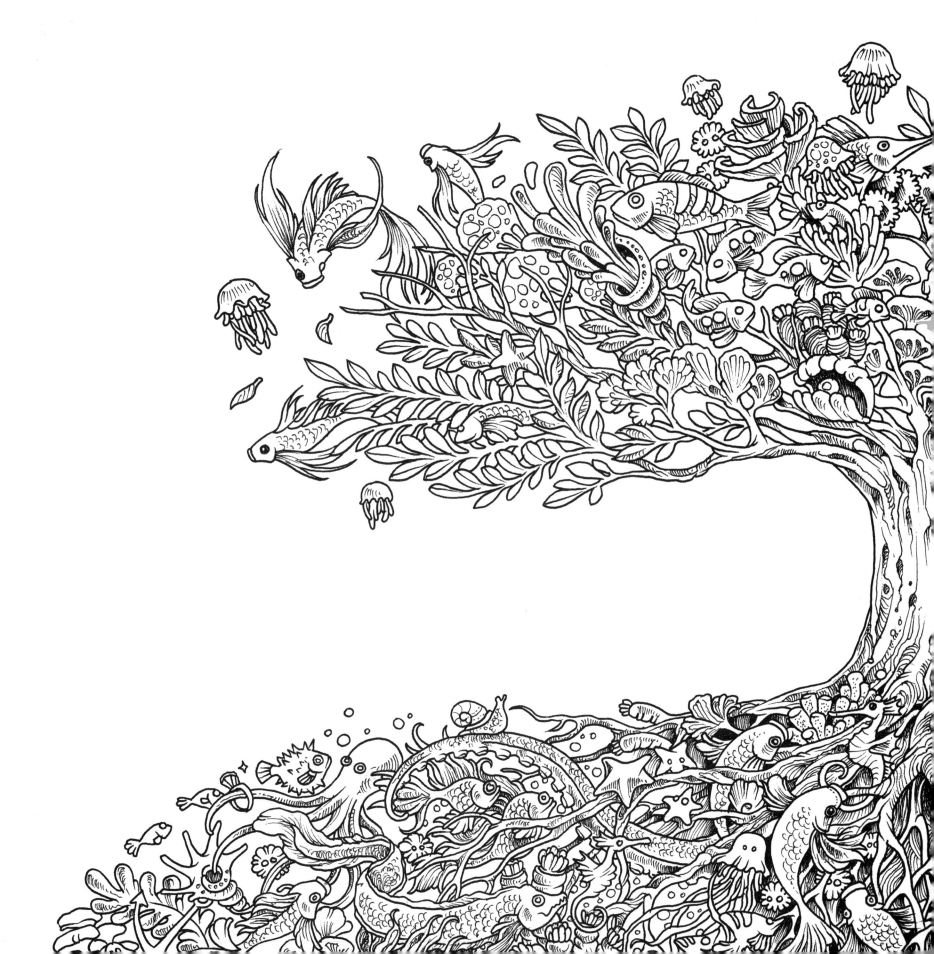

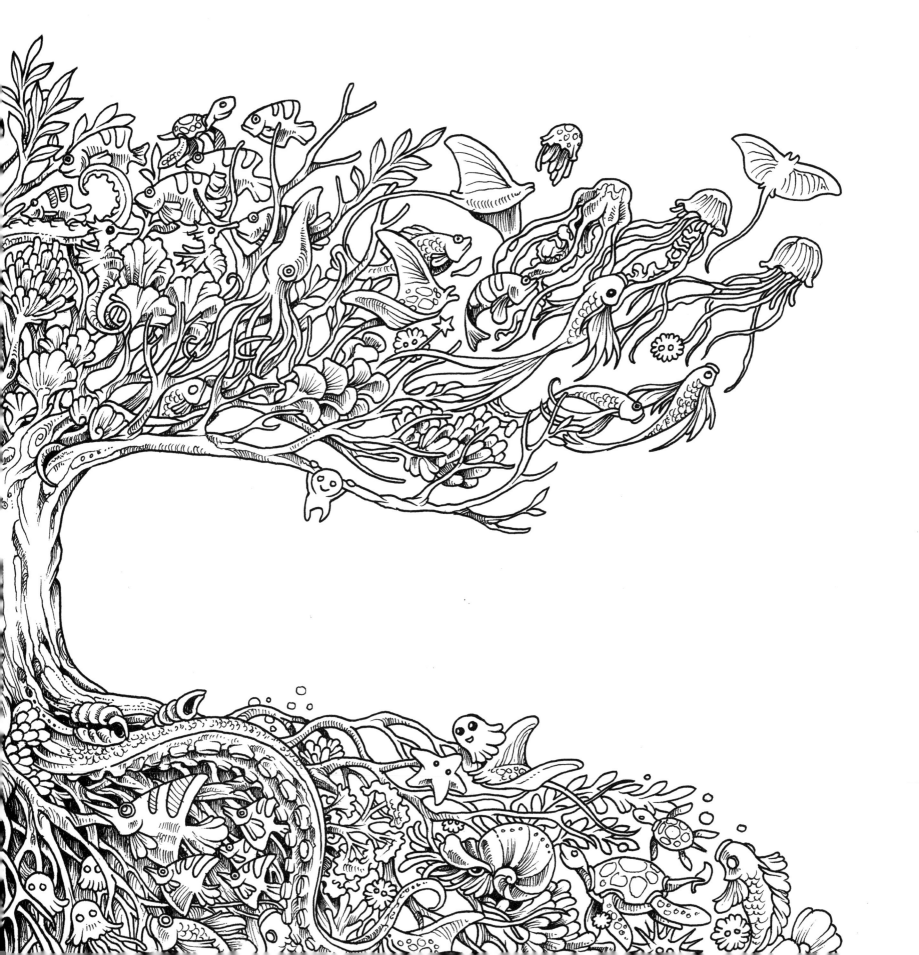

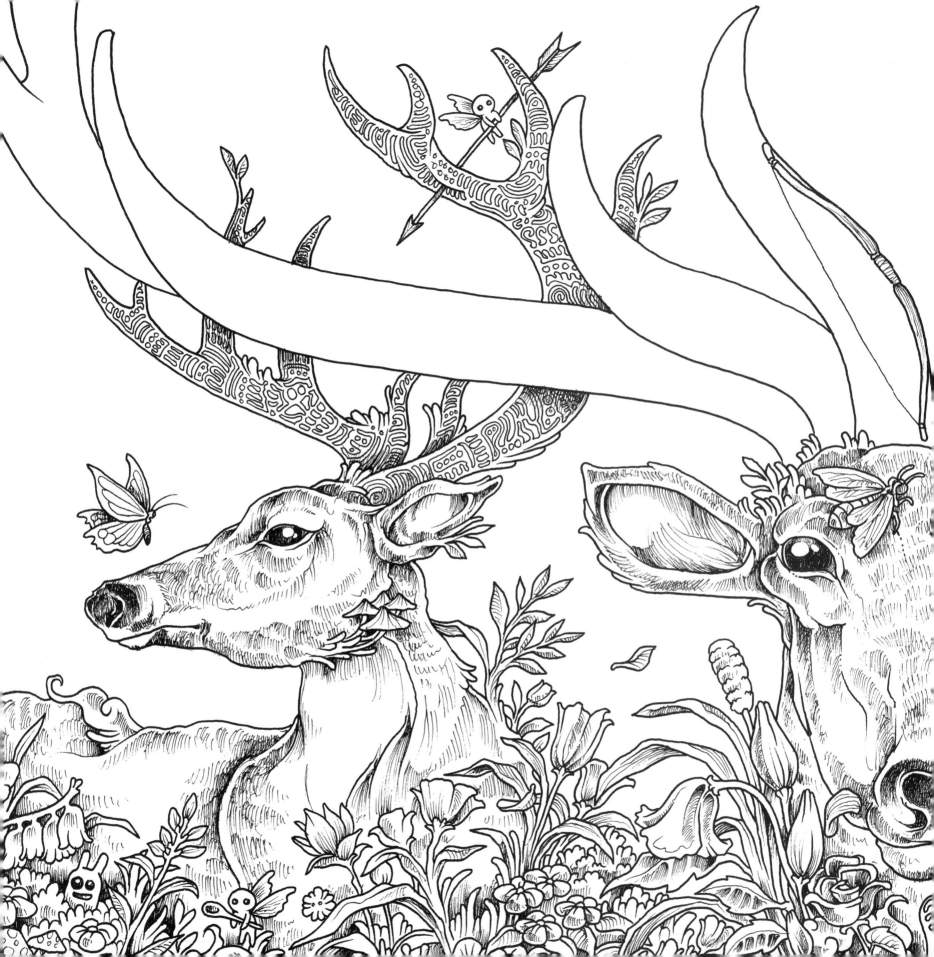

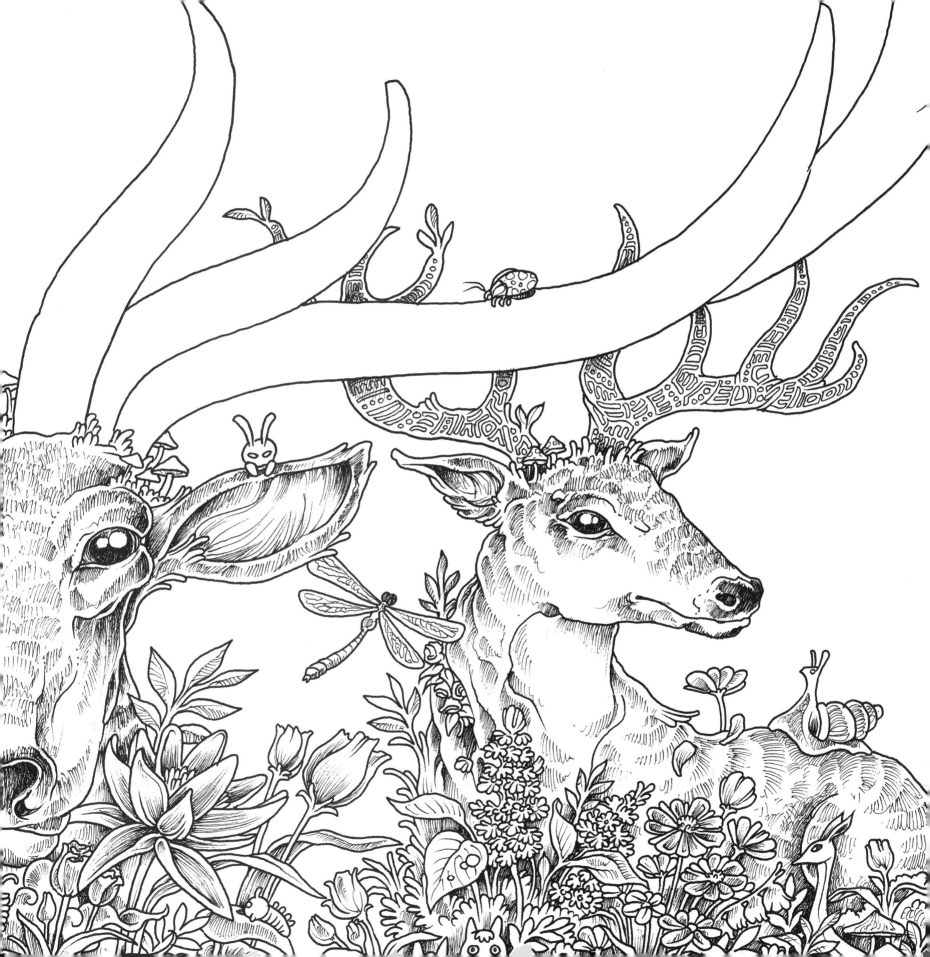

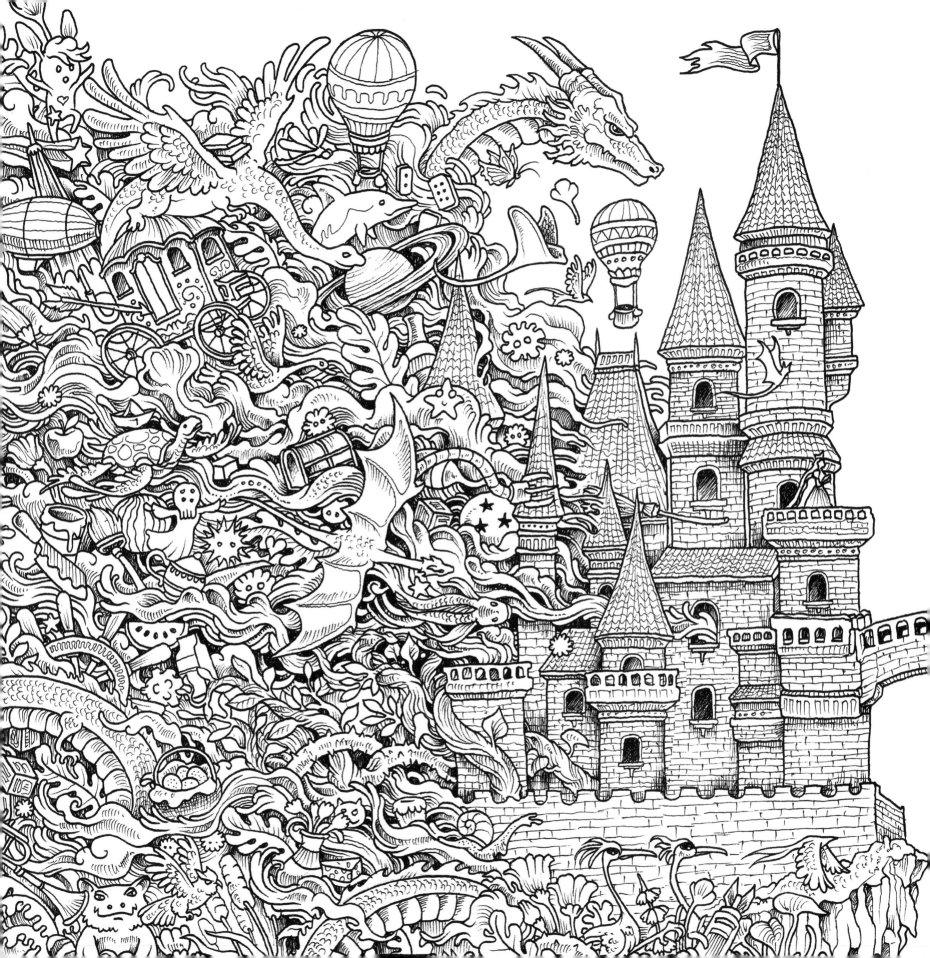

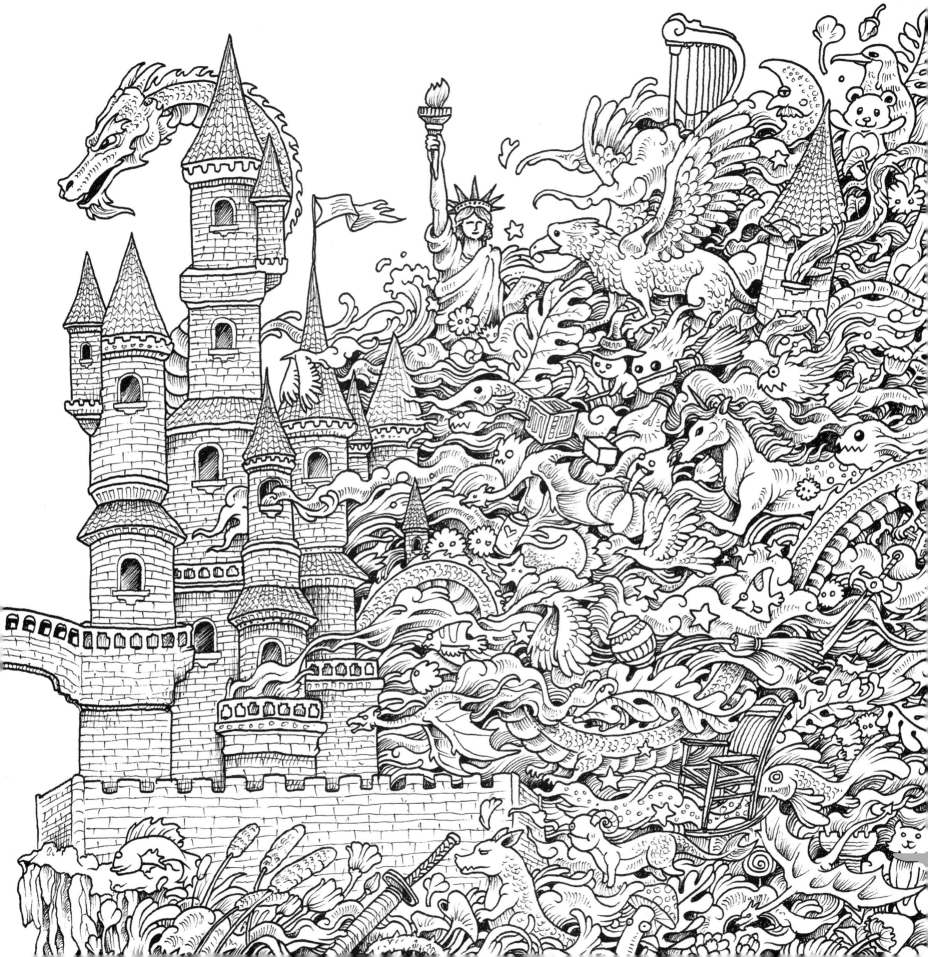

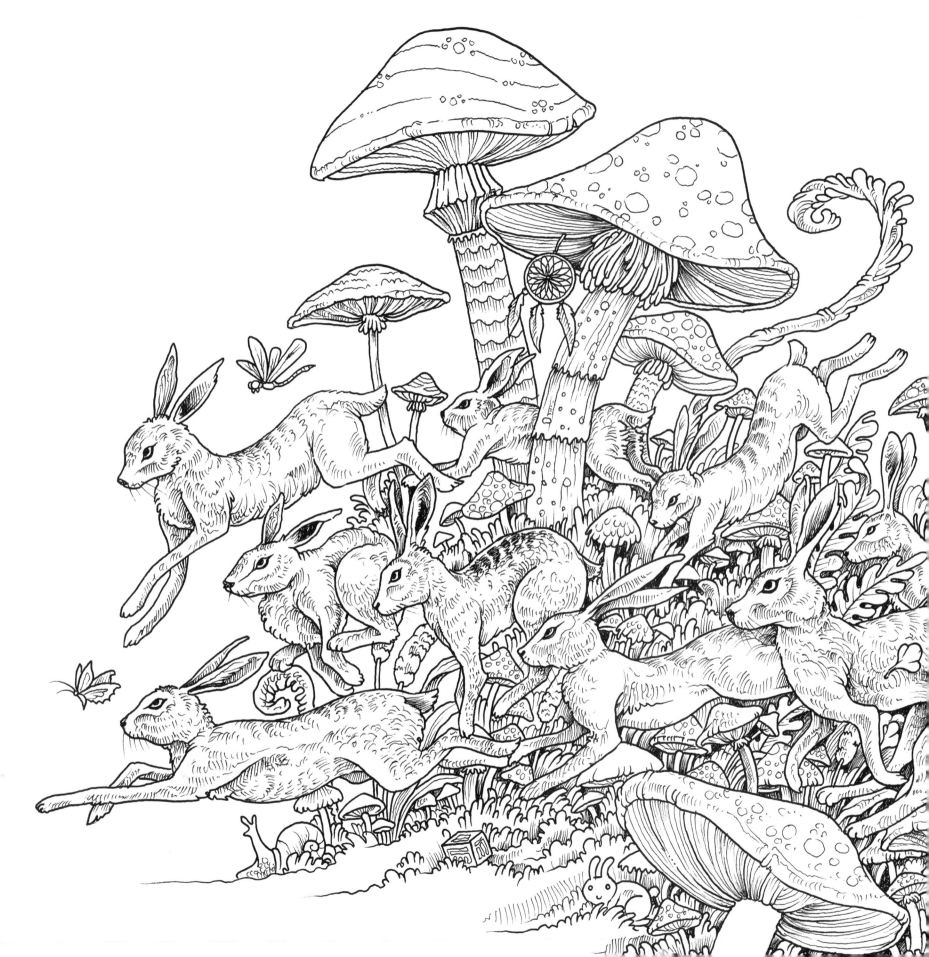

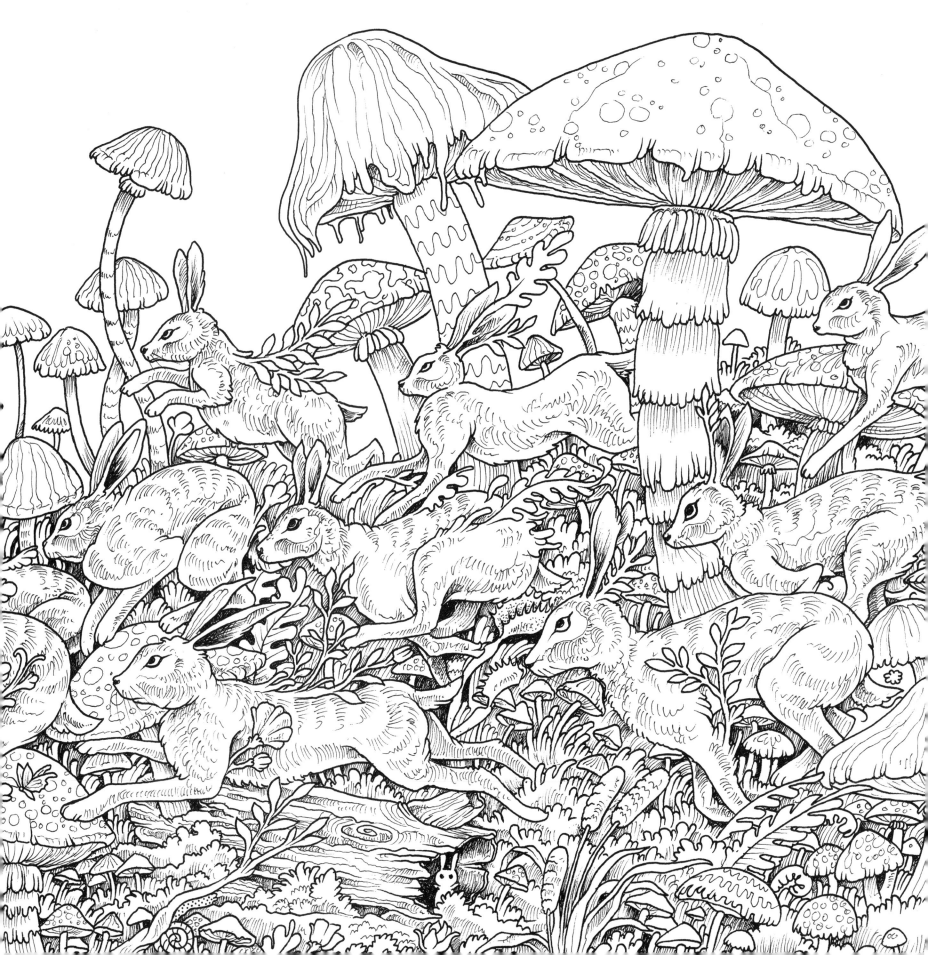

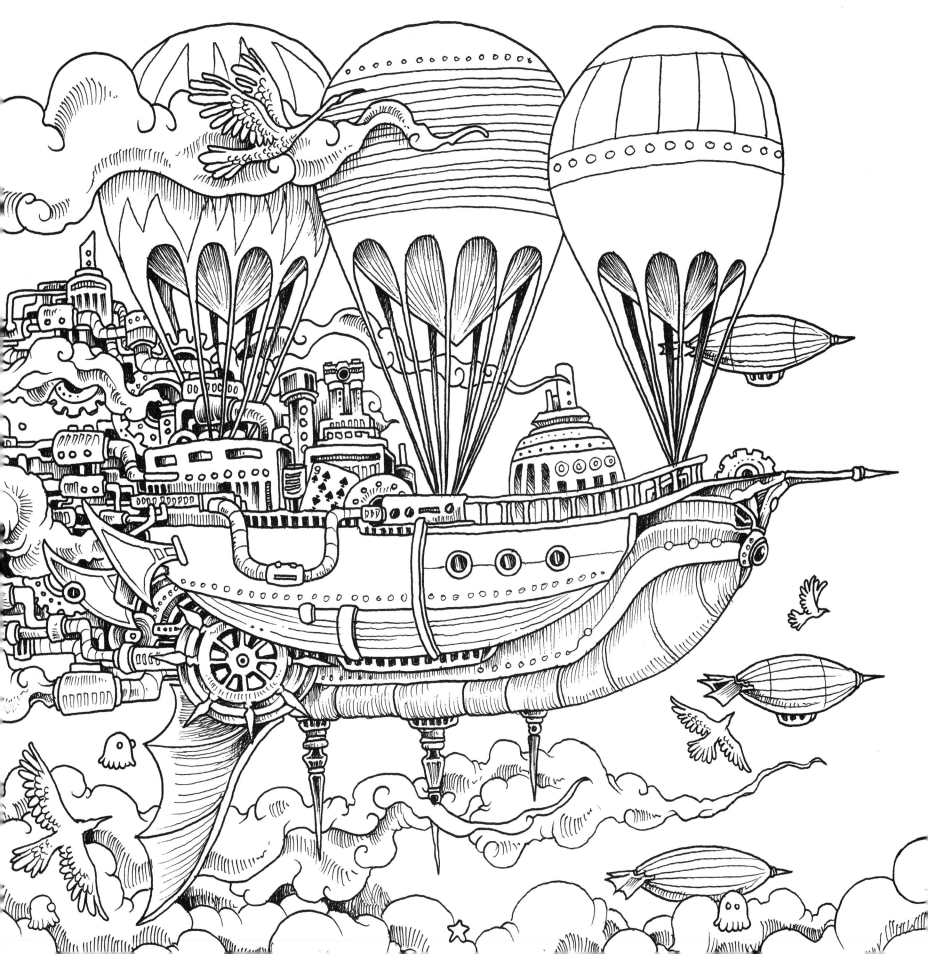

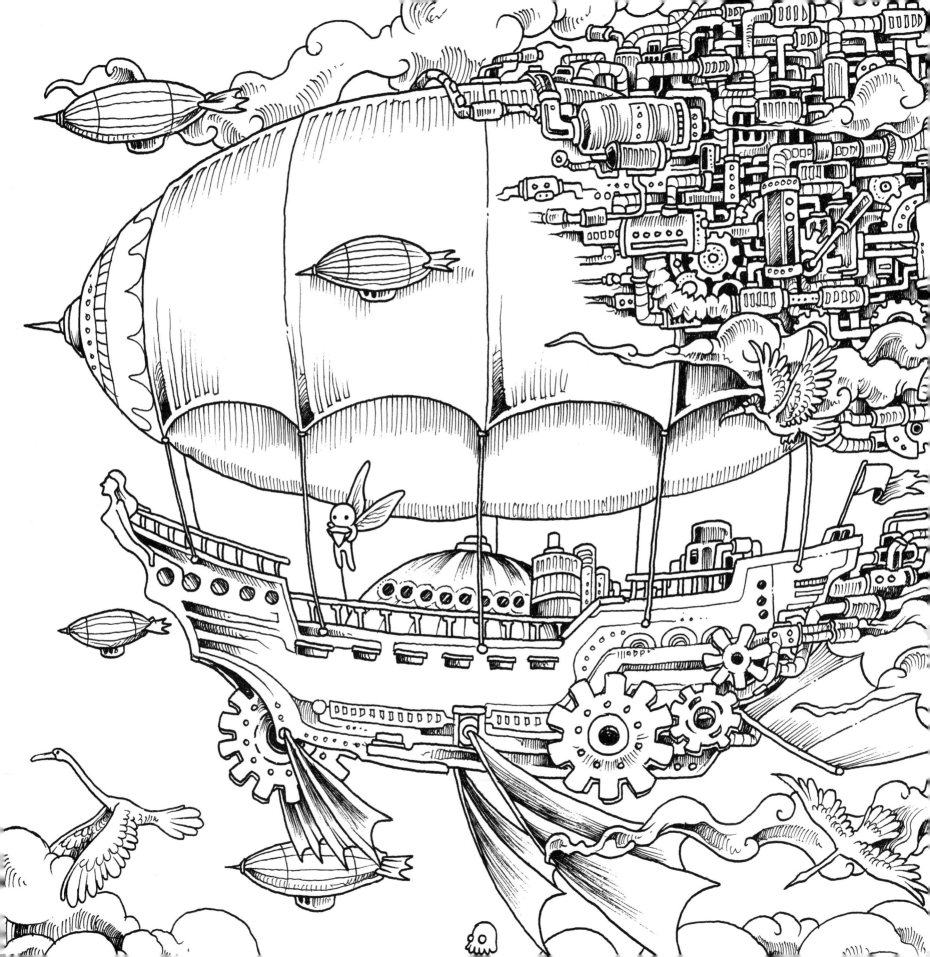

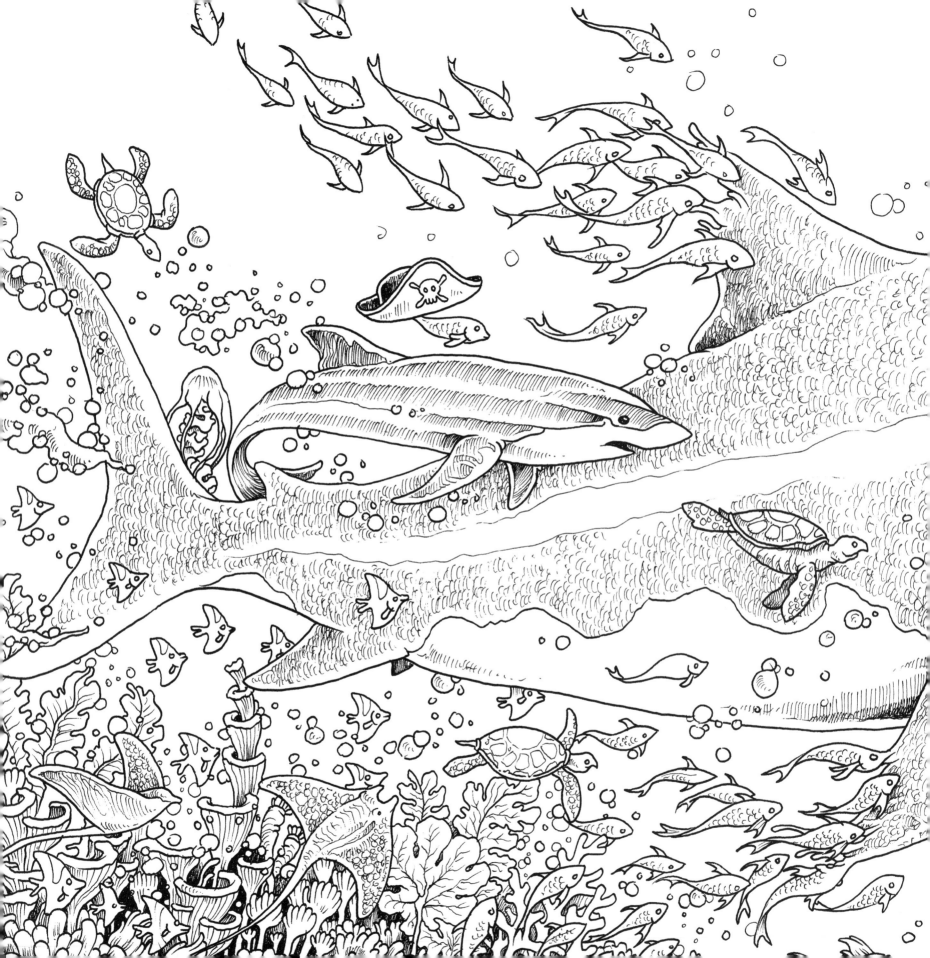

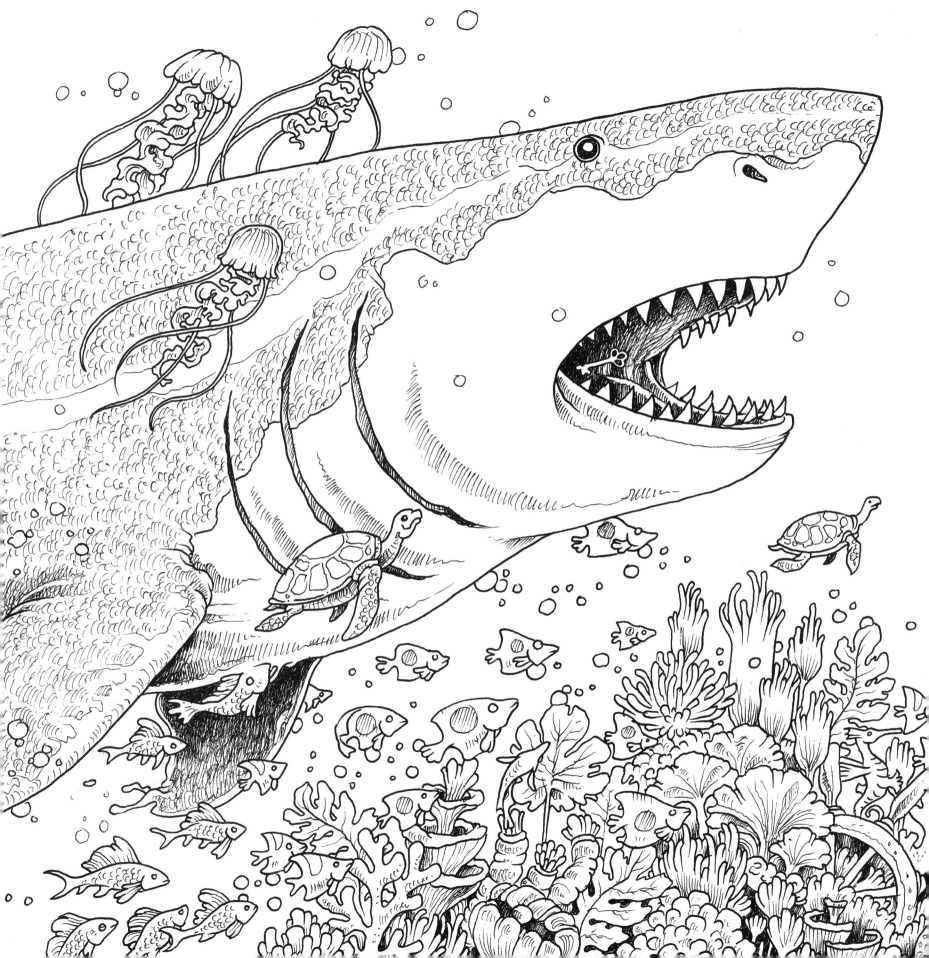

Fill the stripes with intricate patterns.

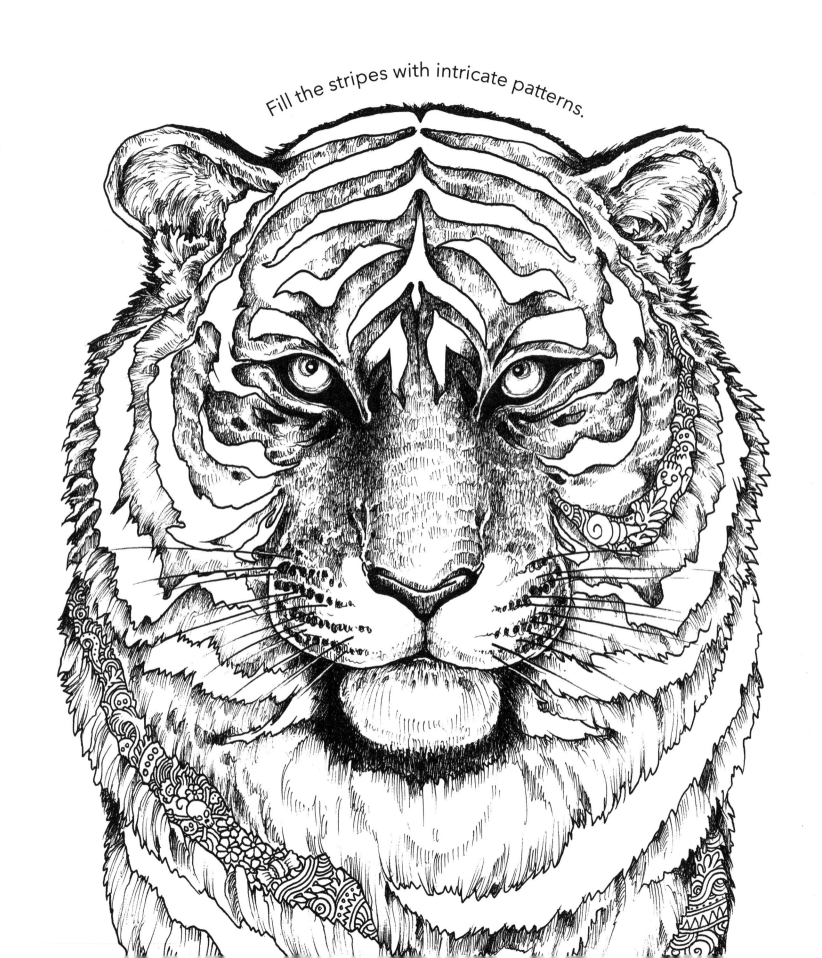

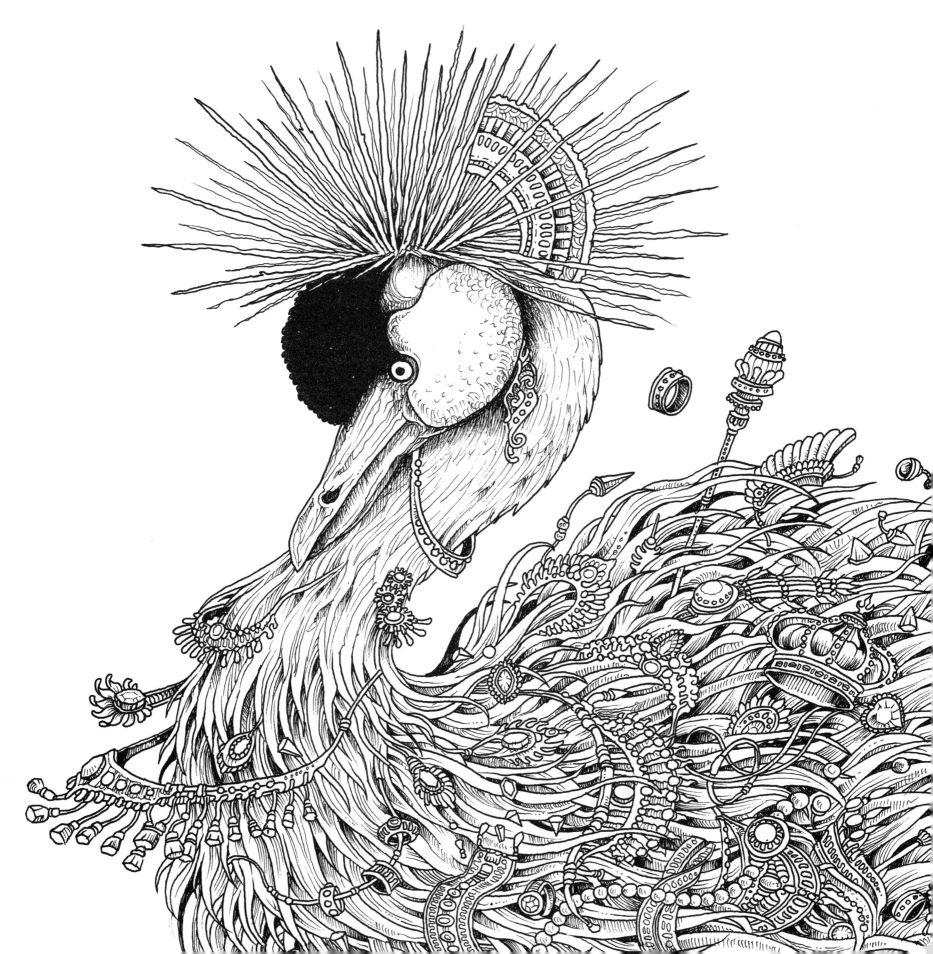

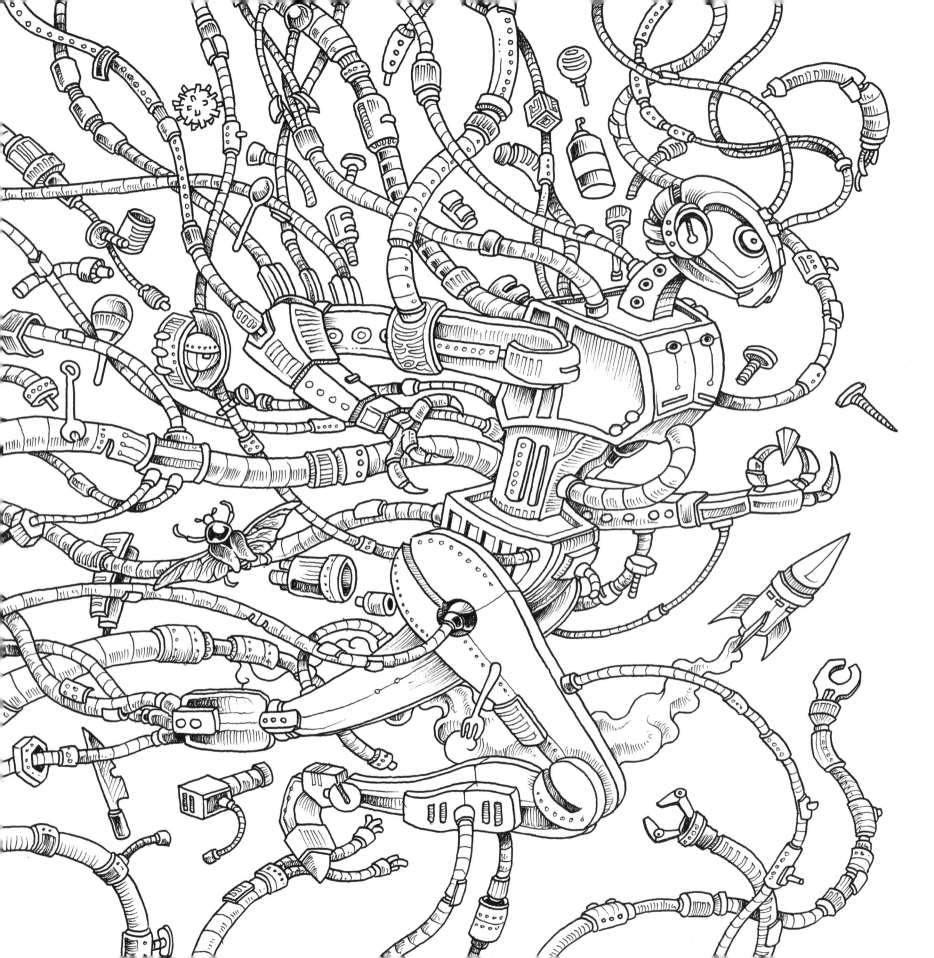

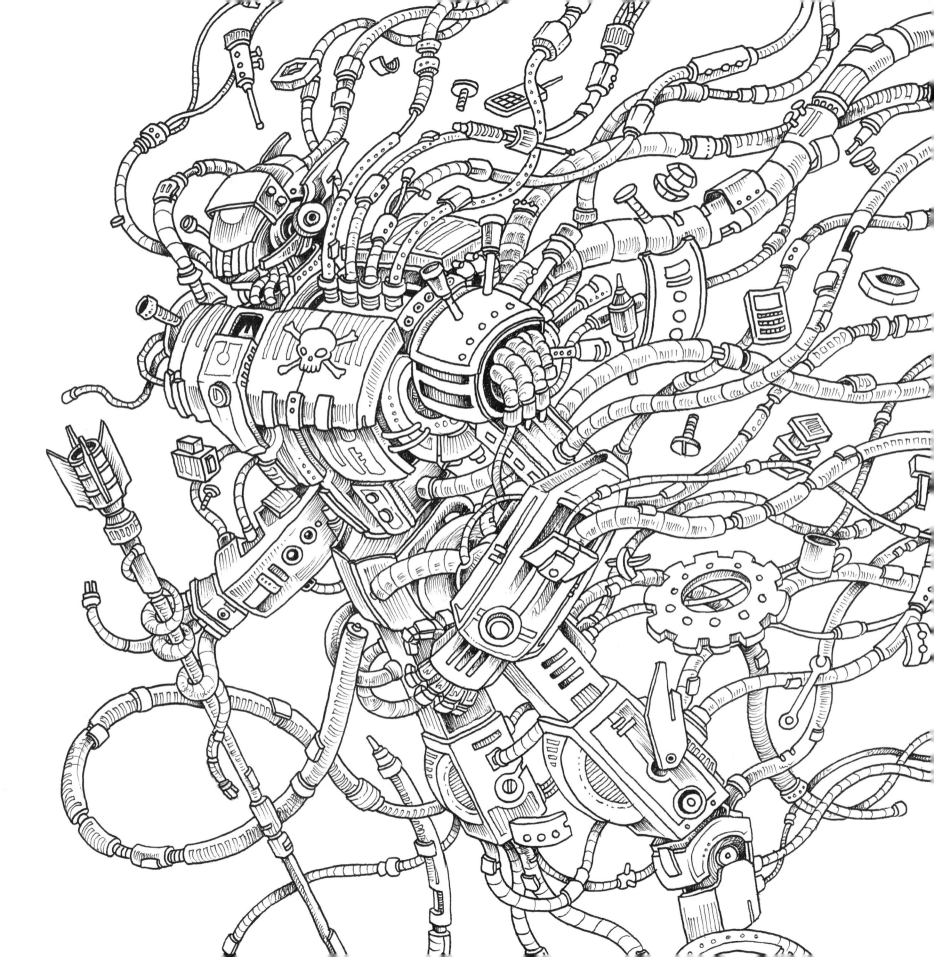

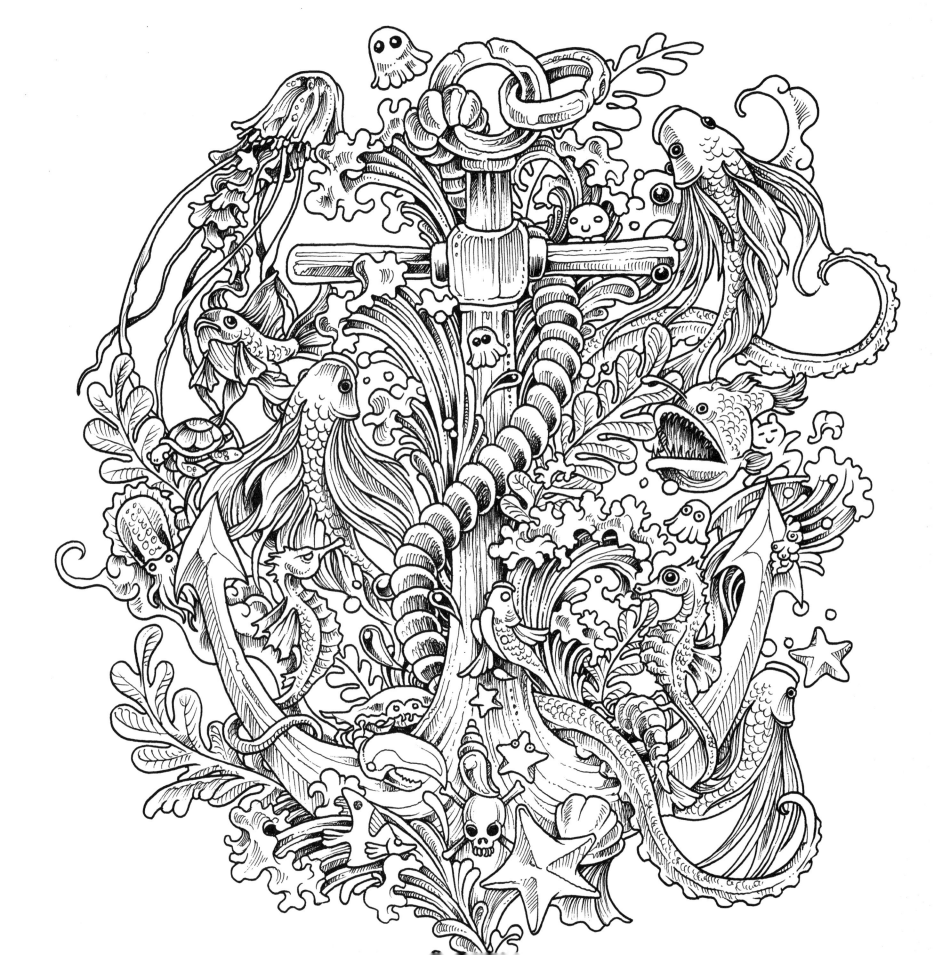

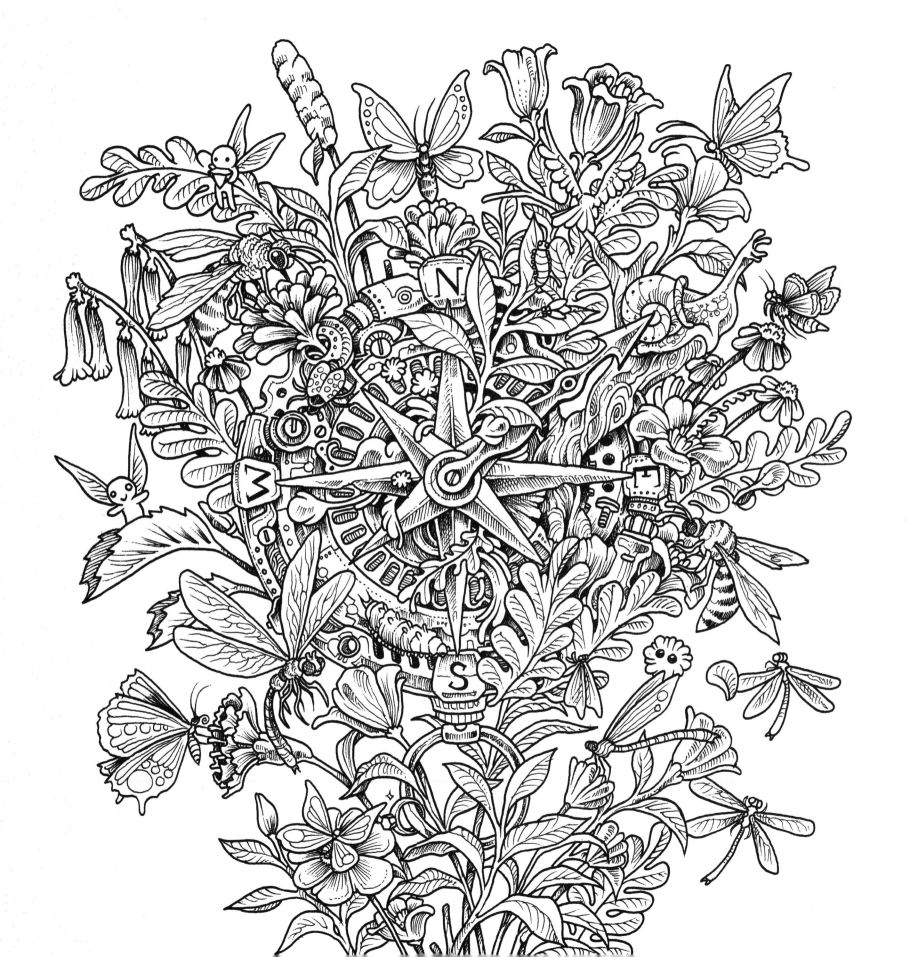

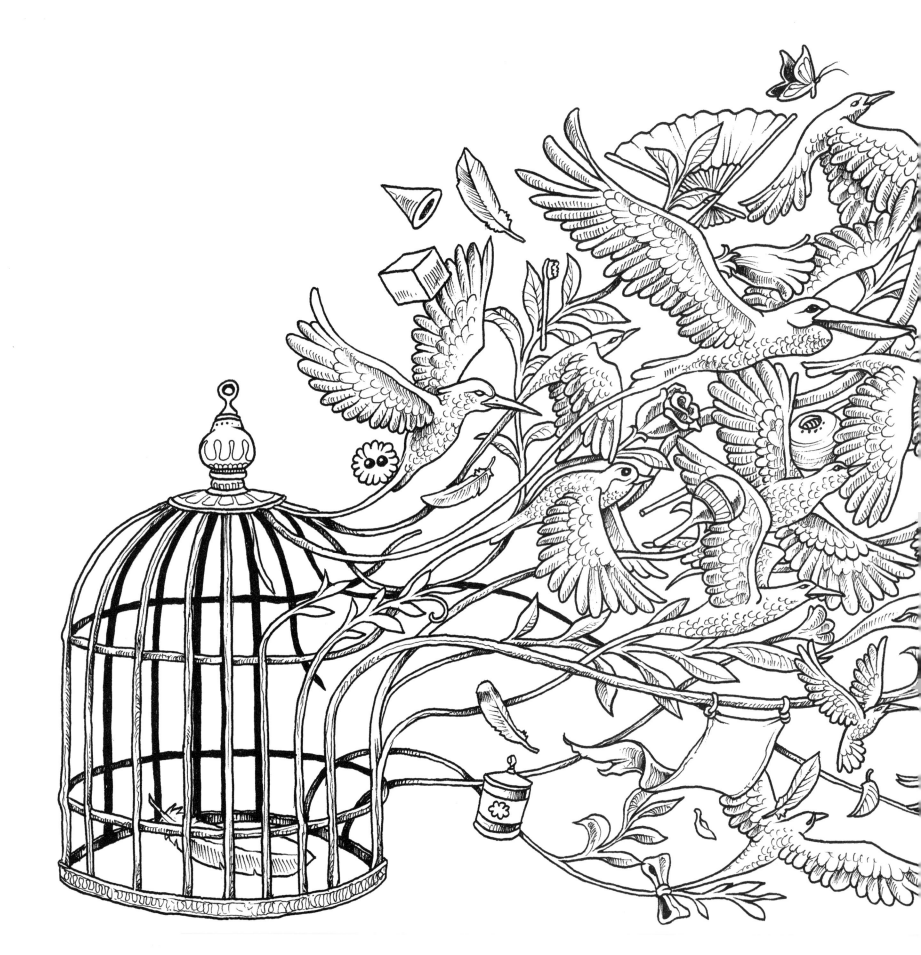

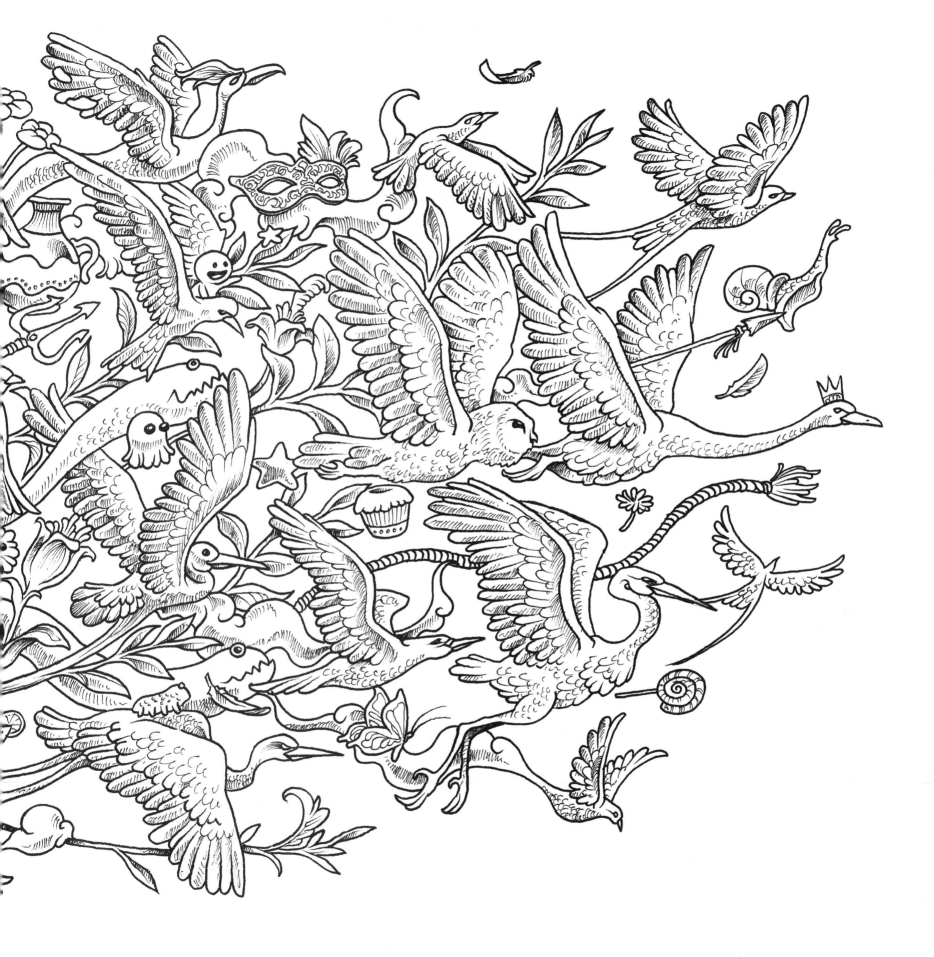

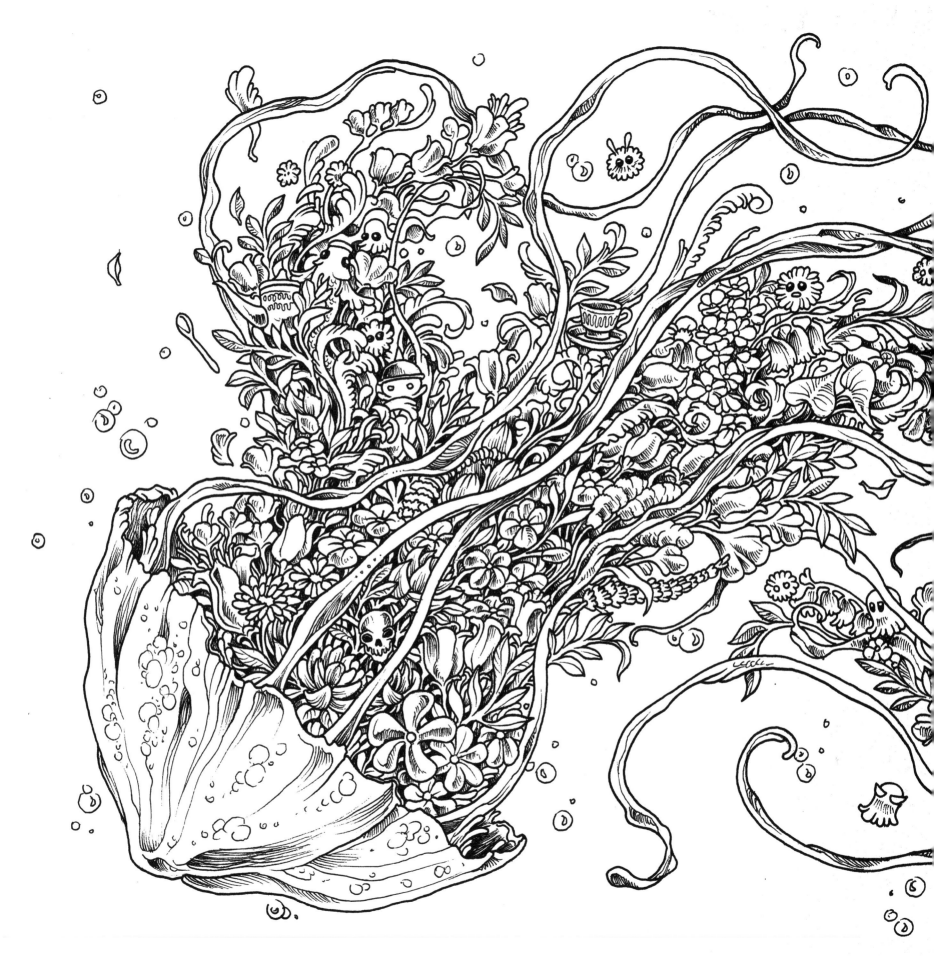

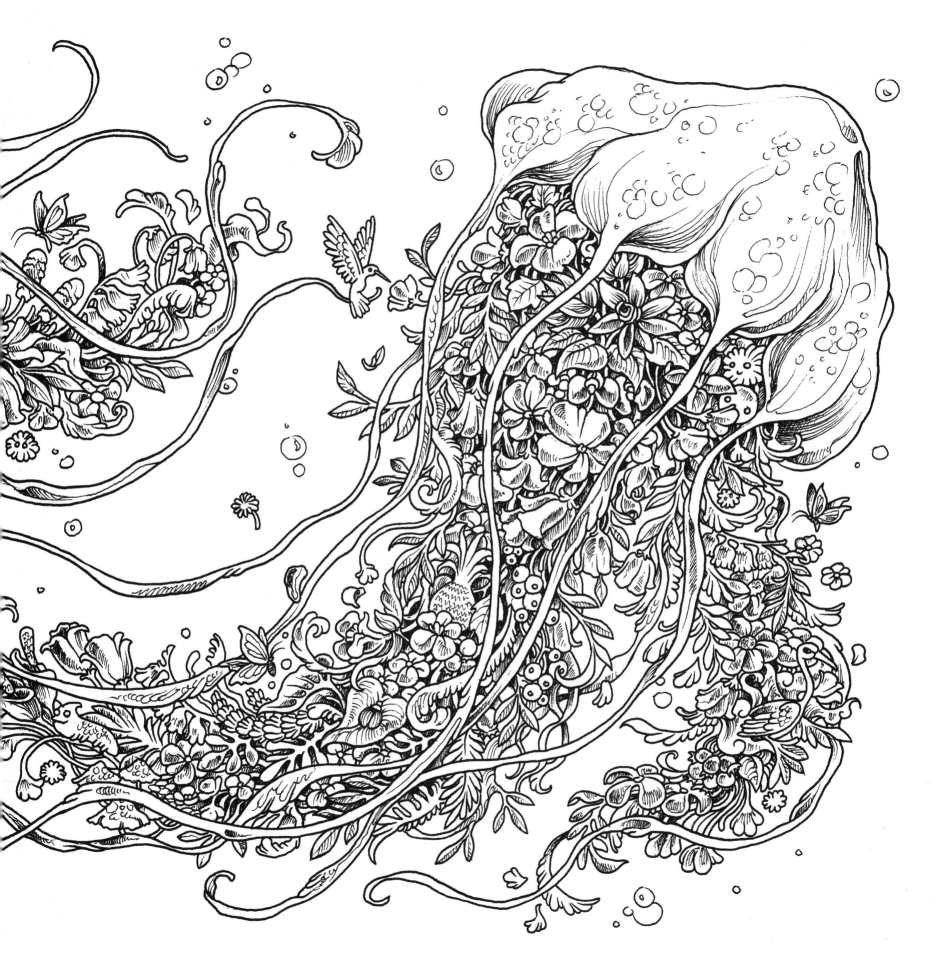

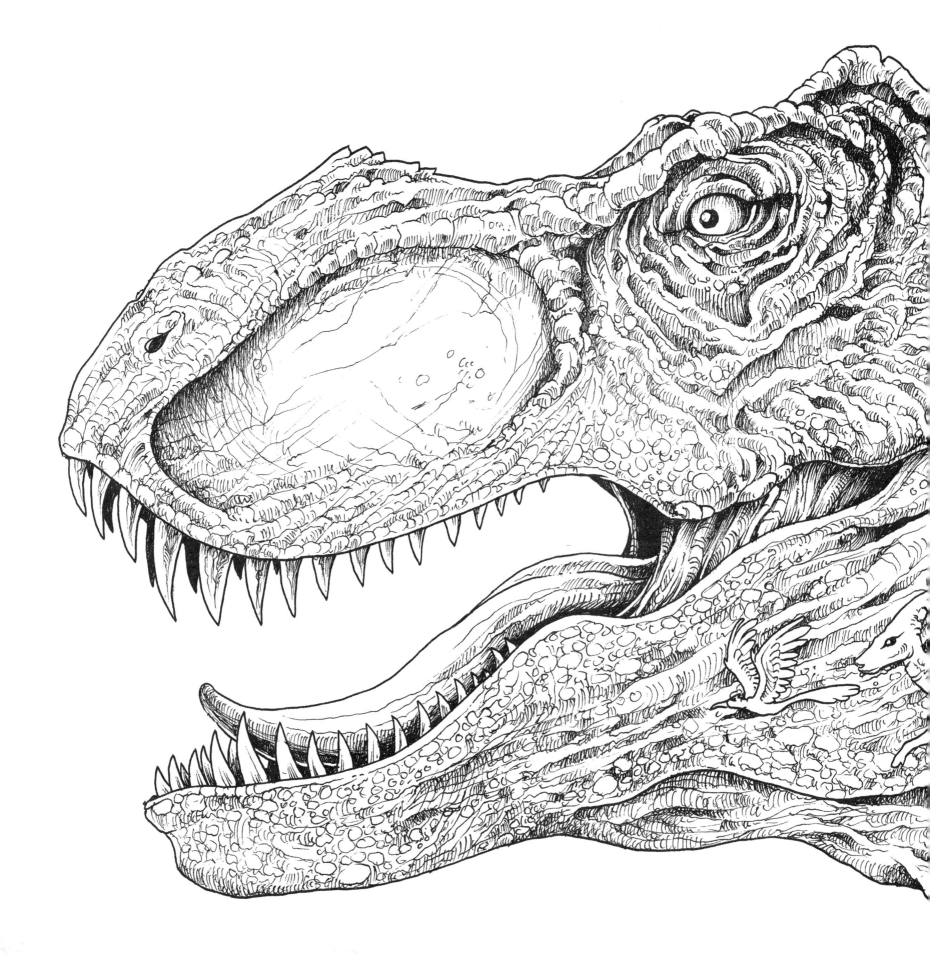

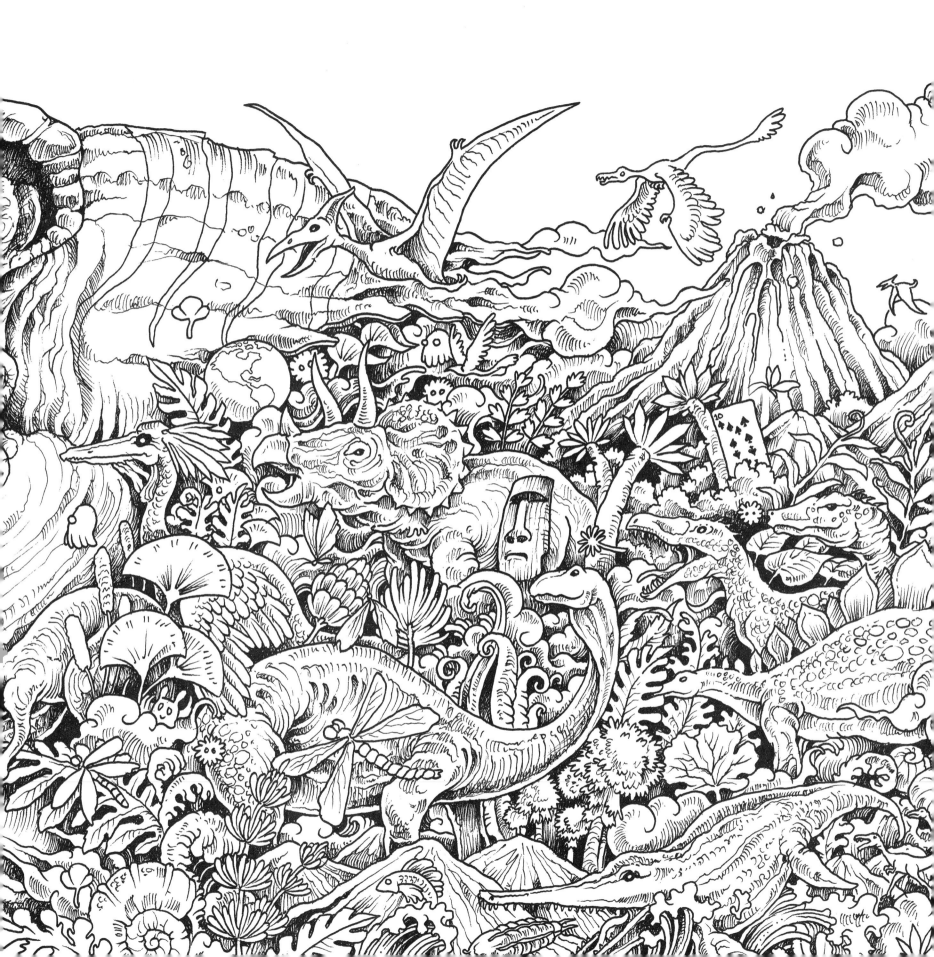

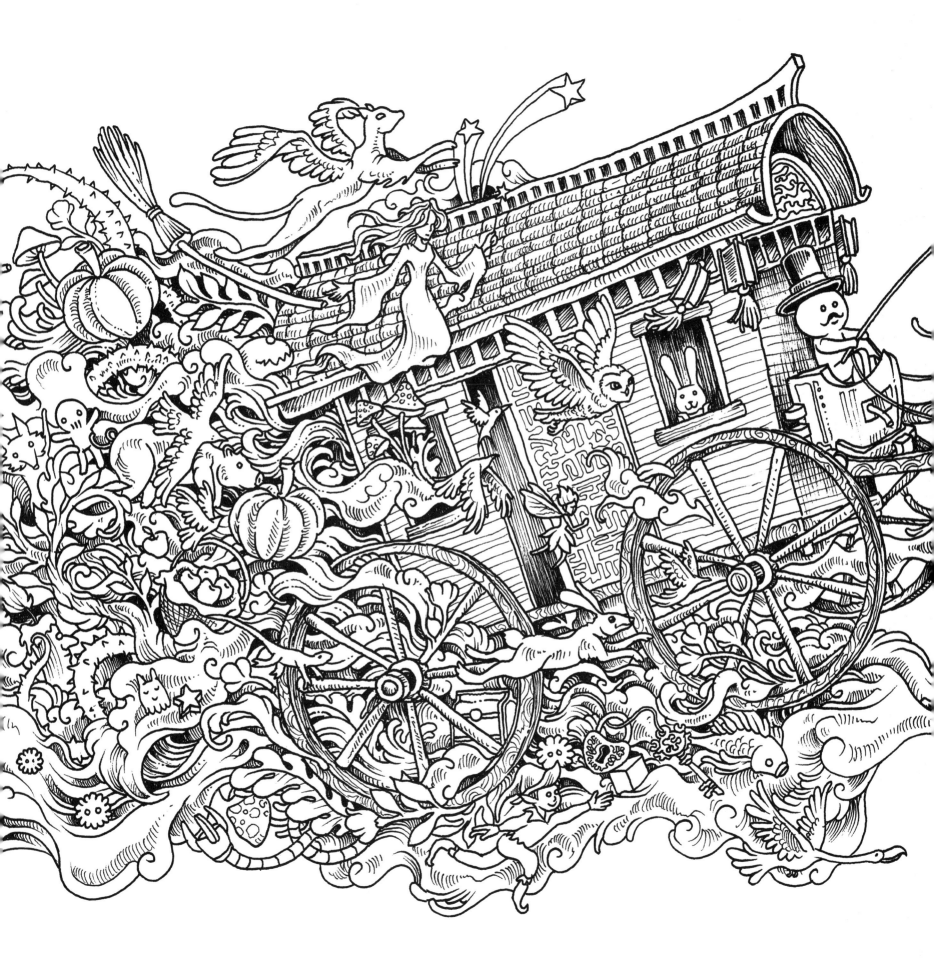

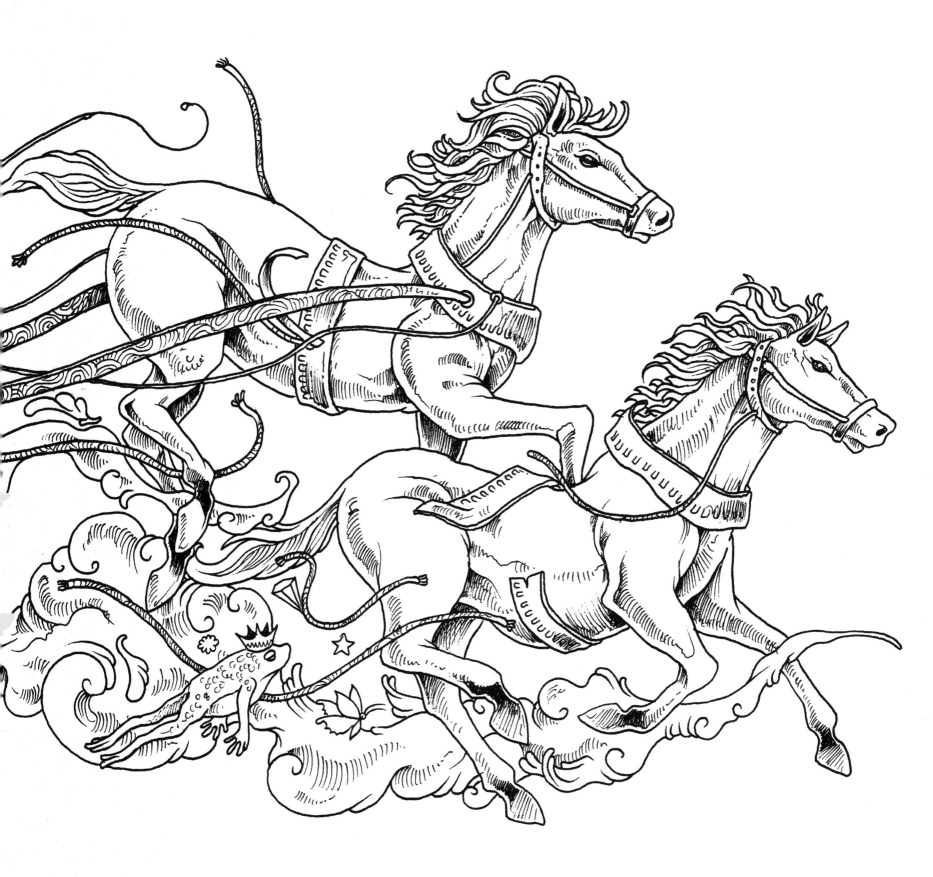

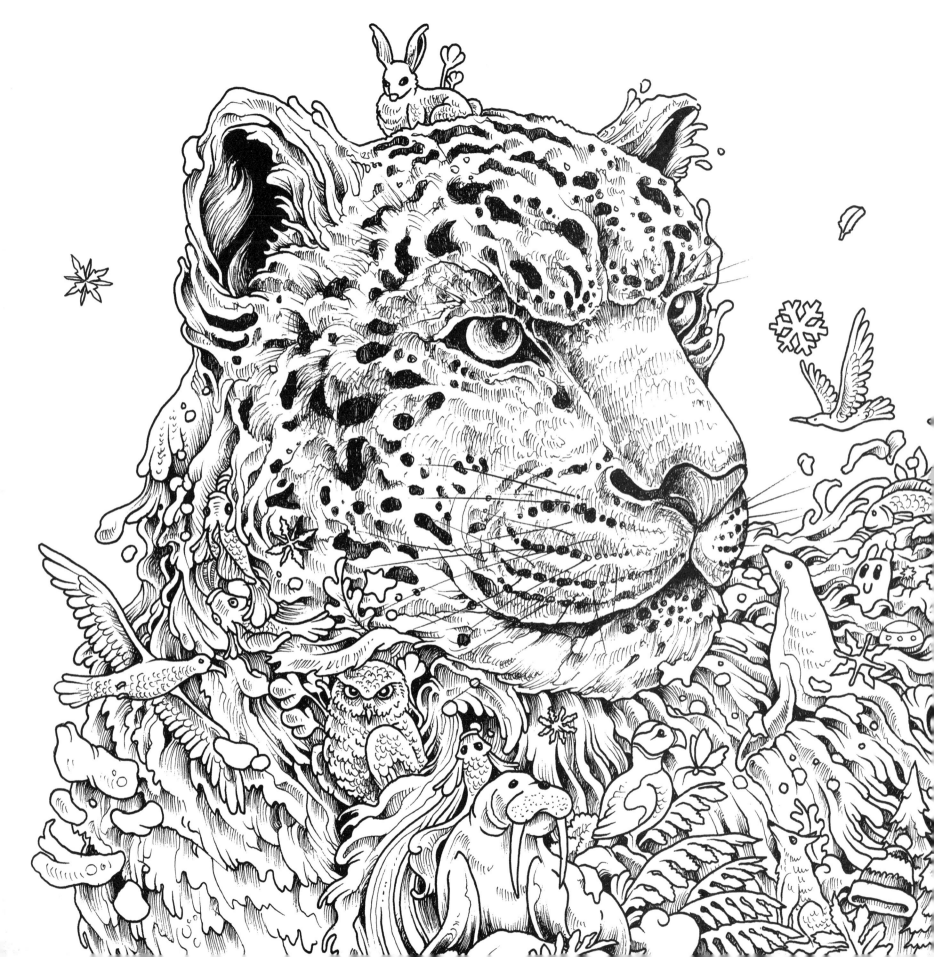

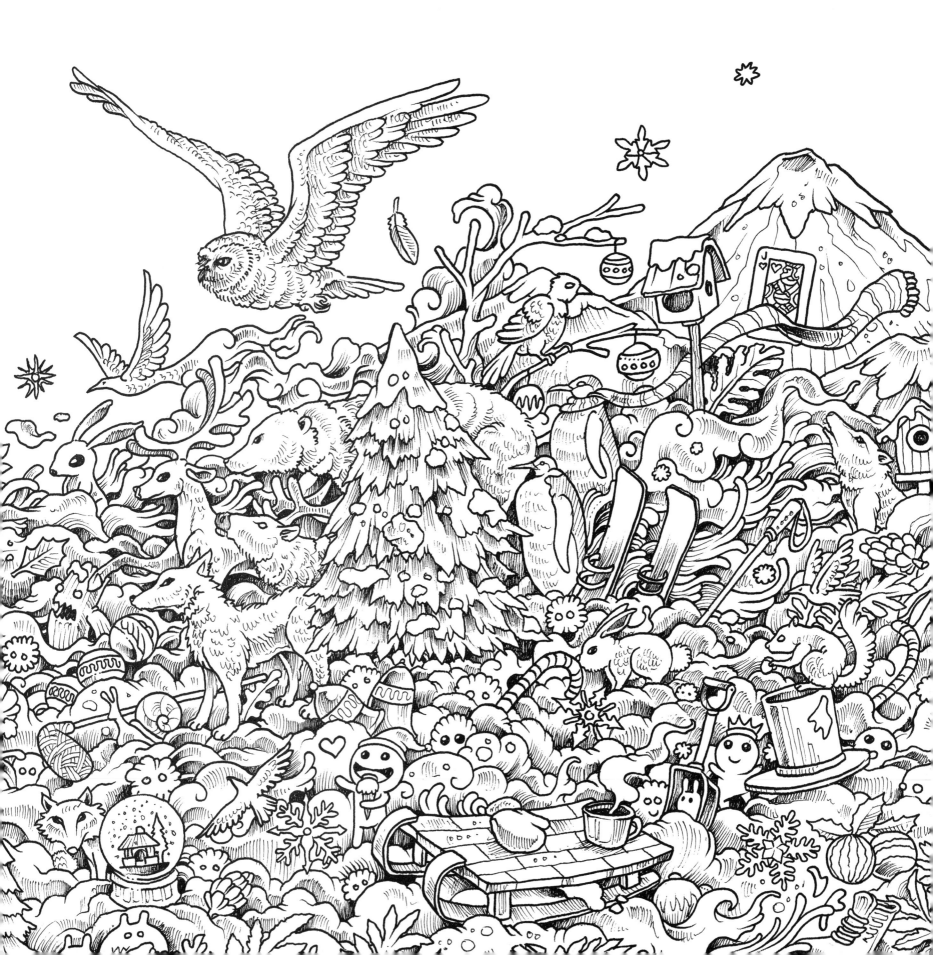

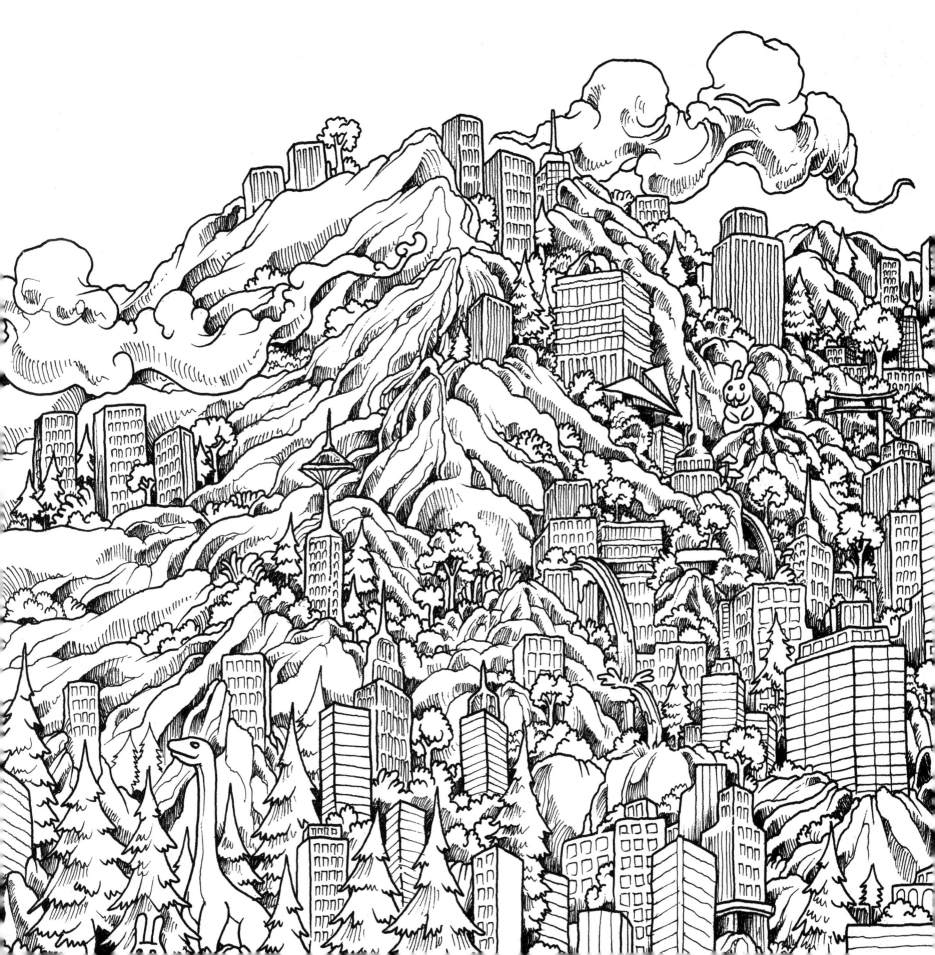

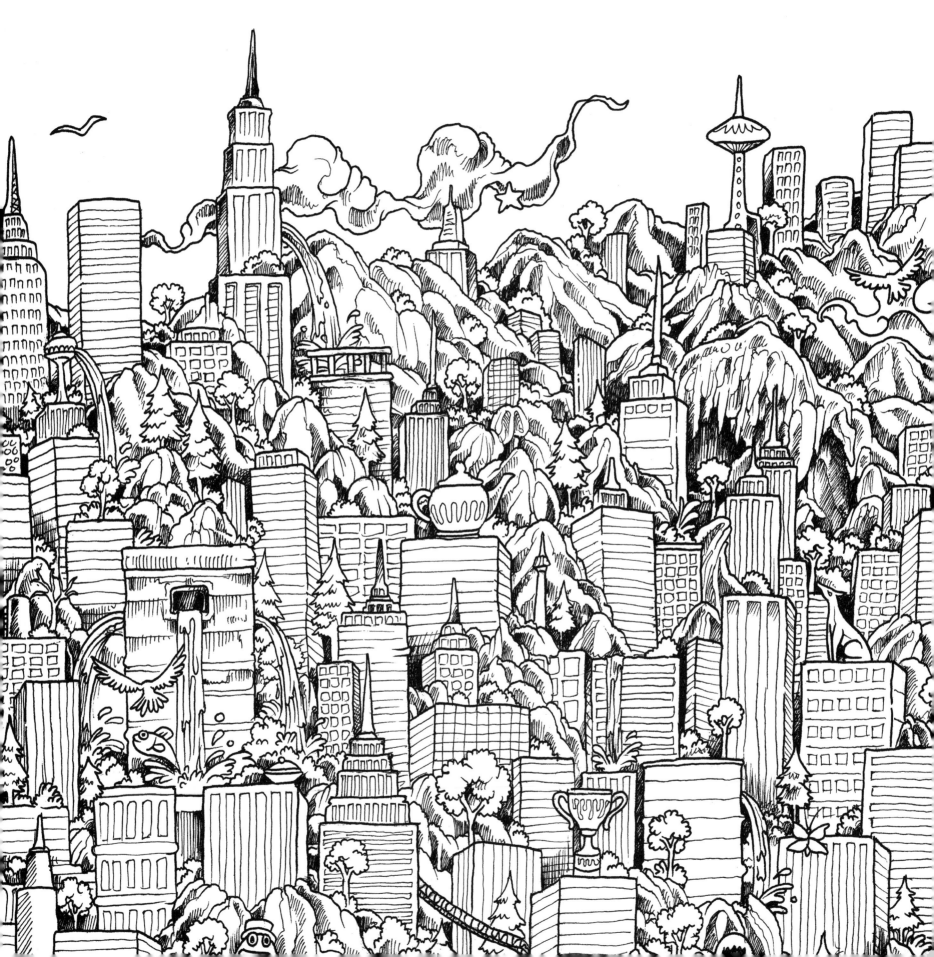

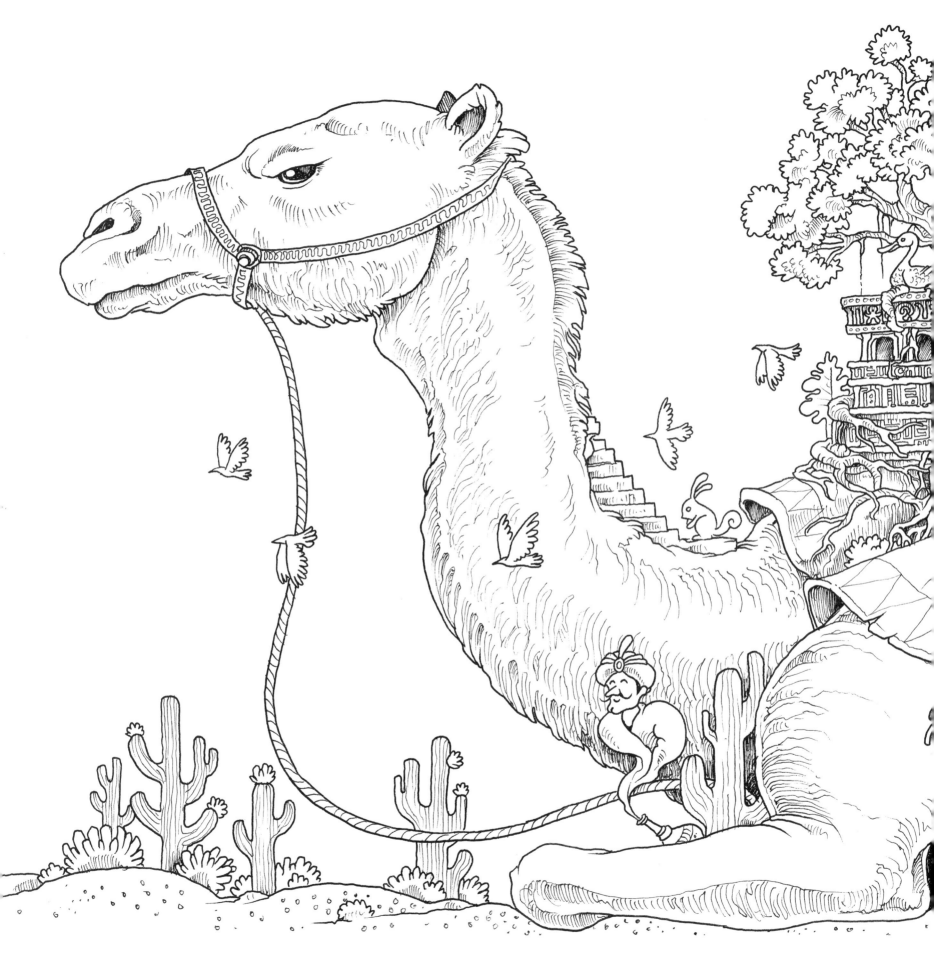

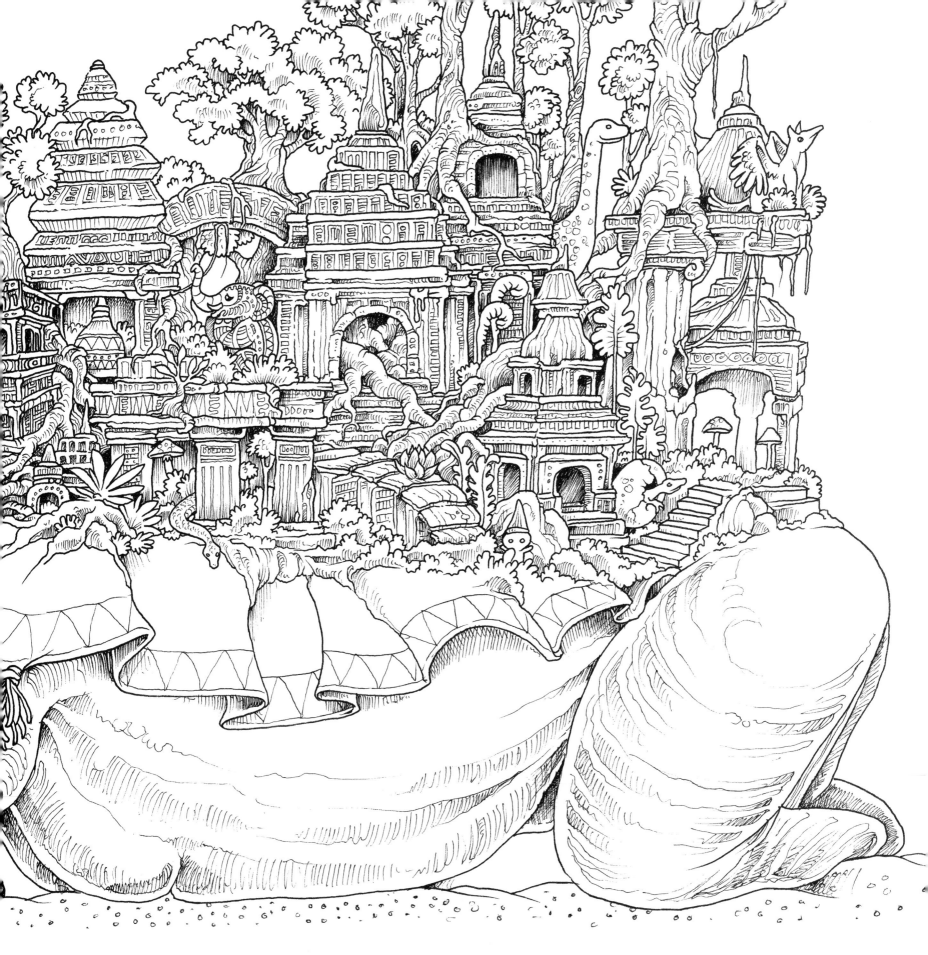

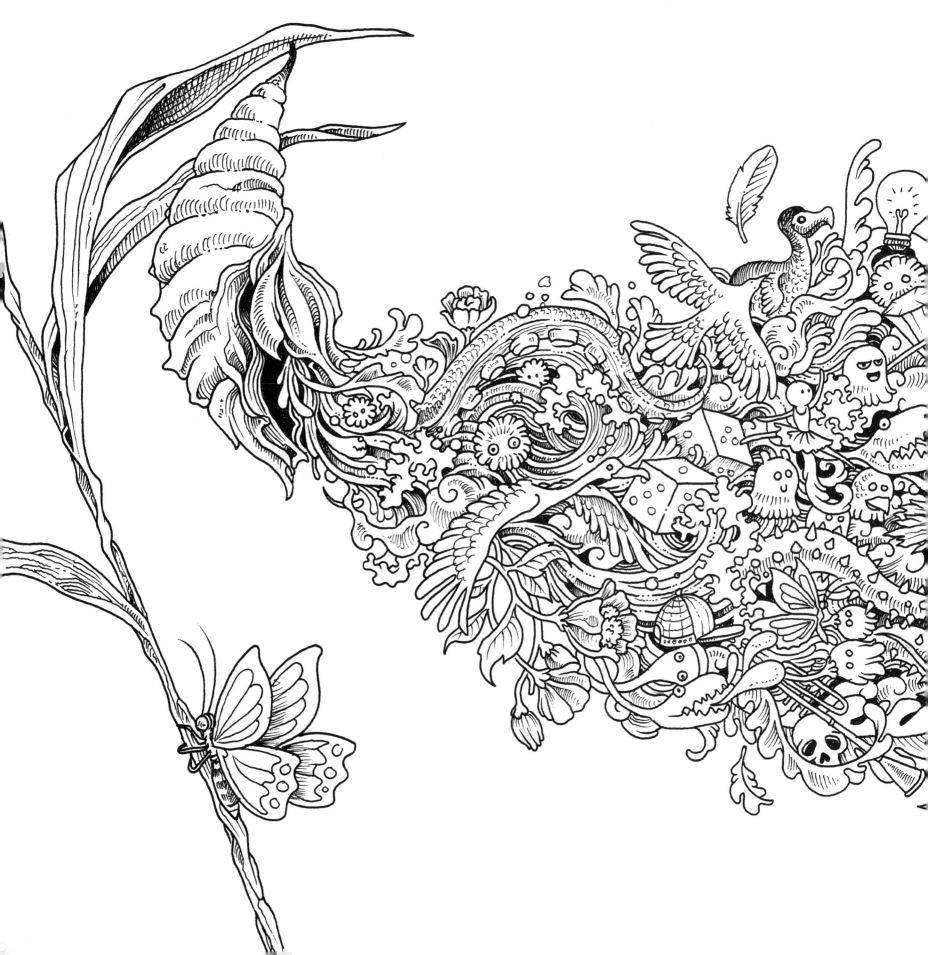

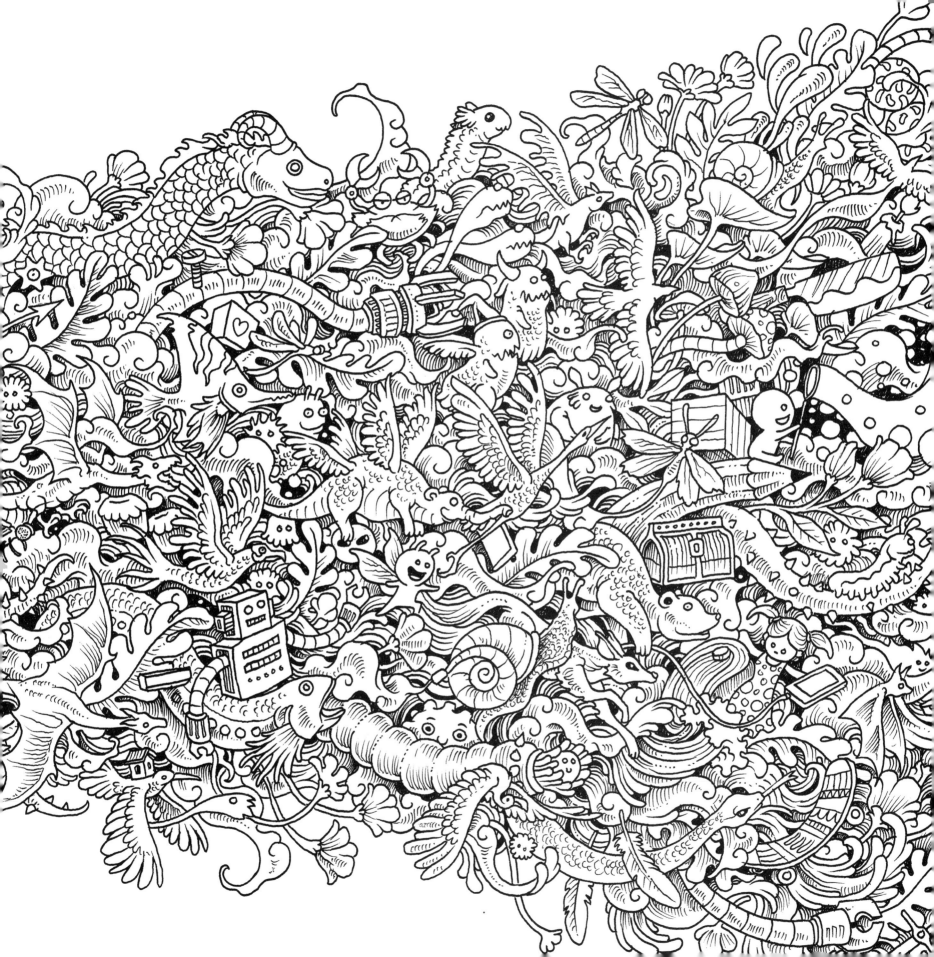

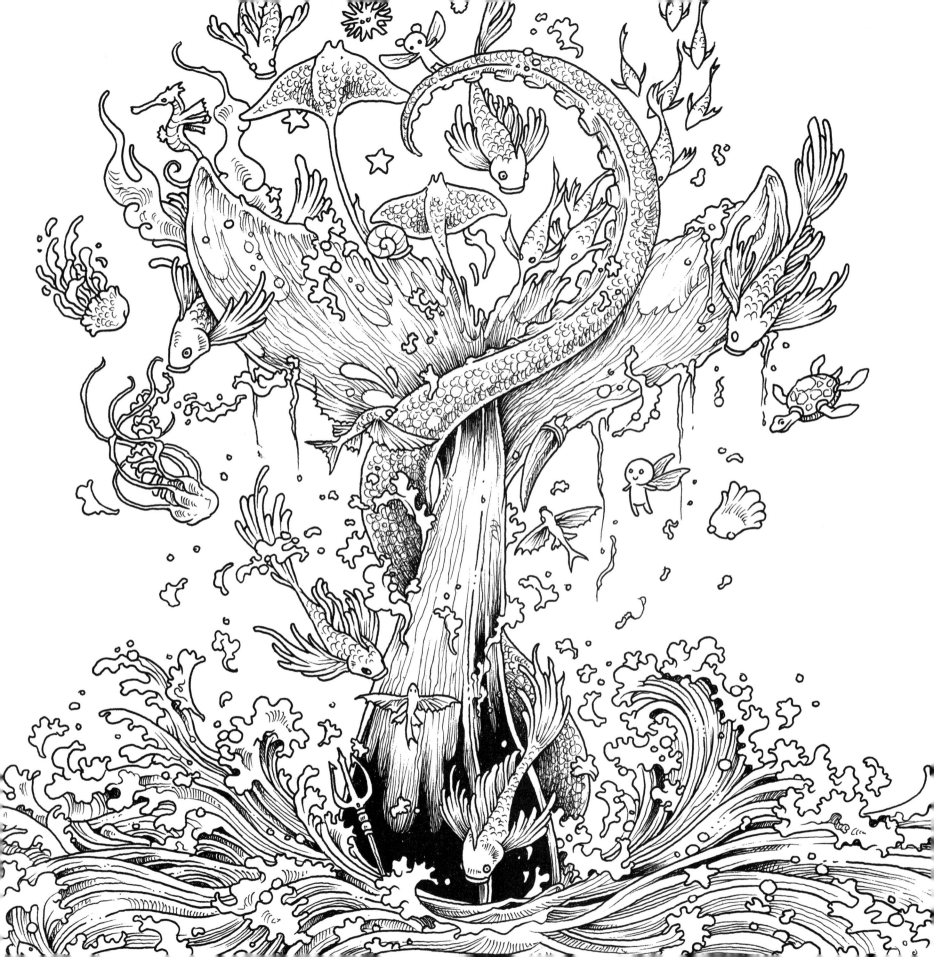

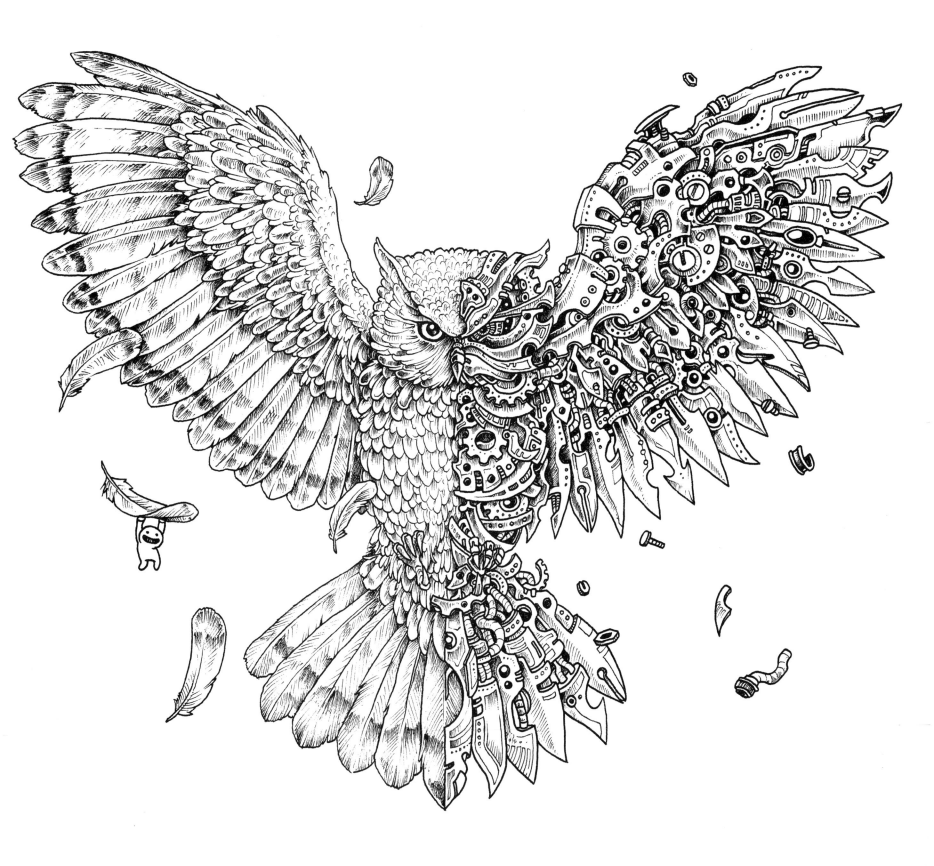

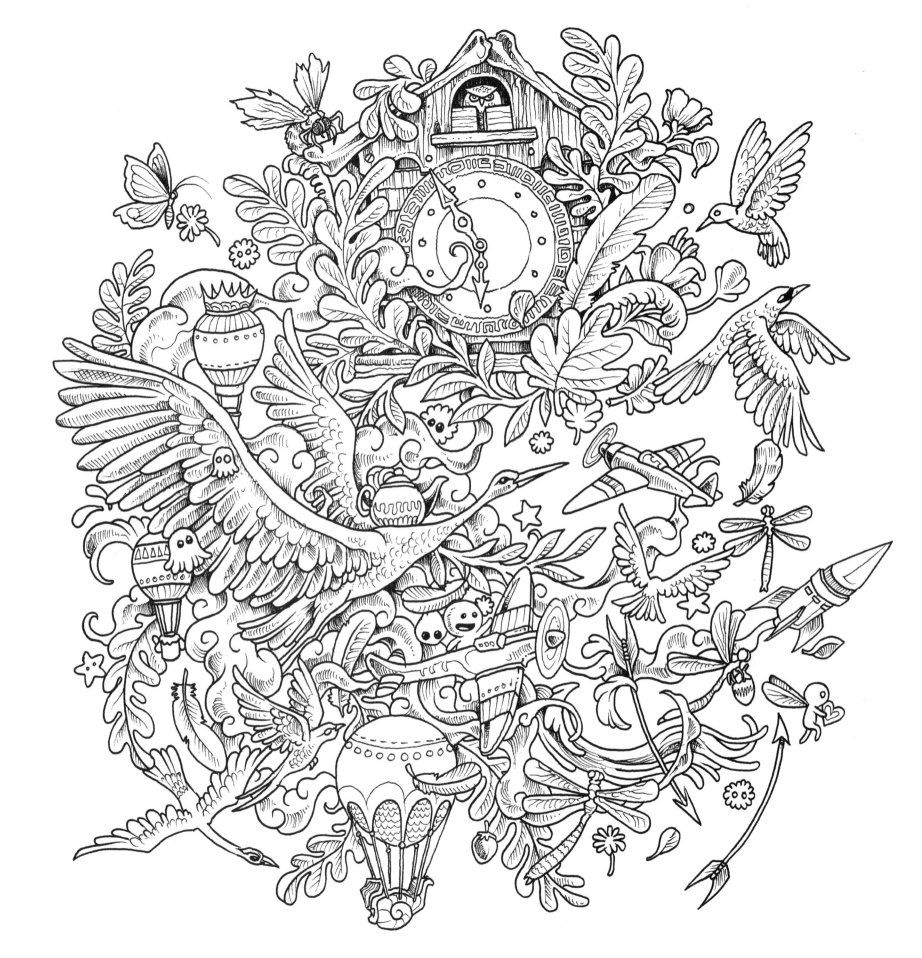

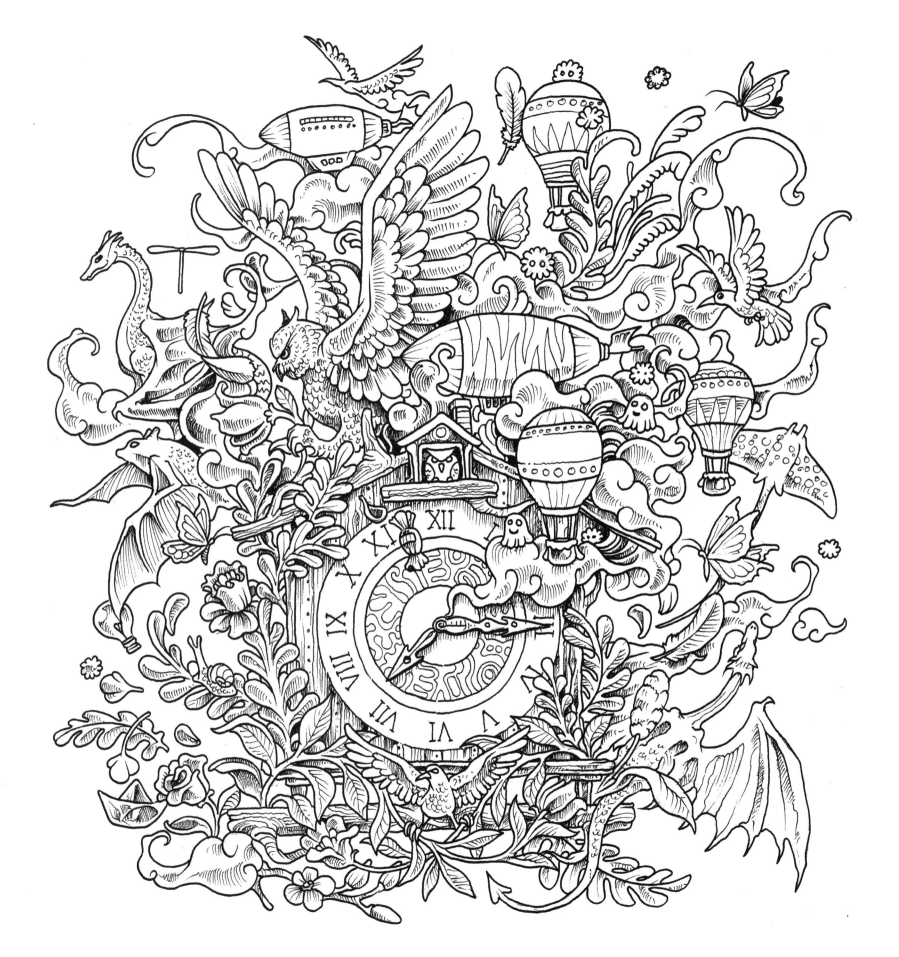

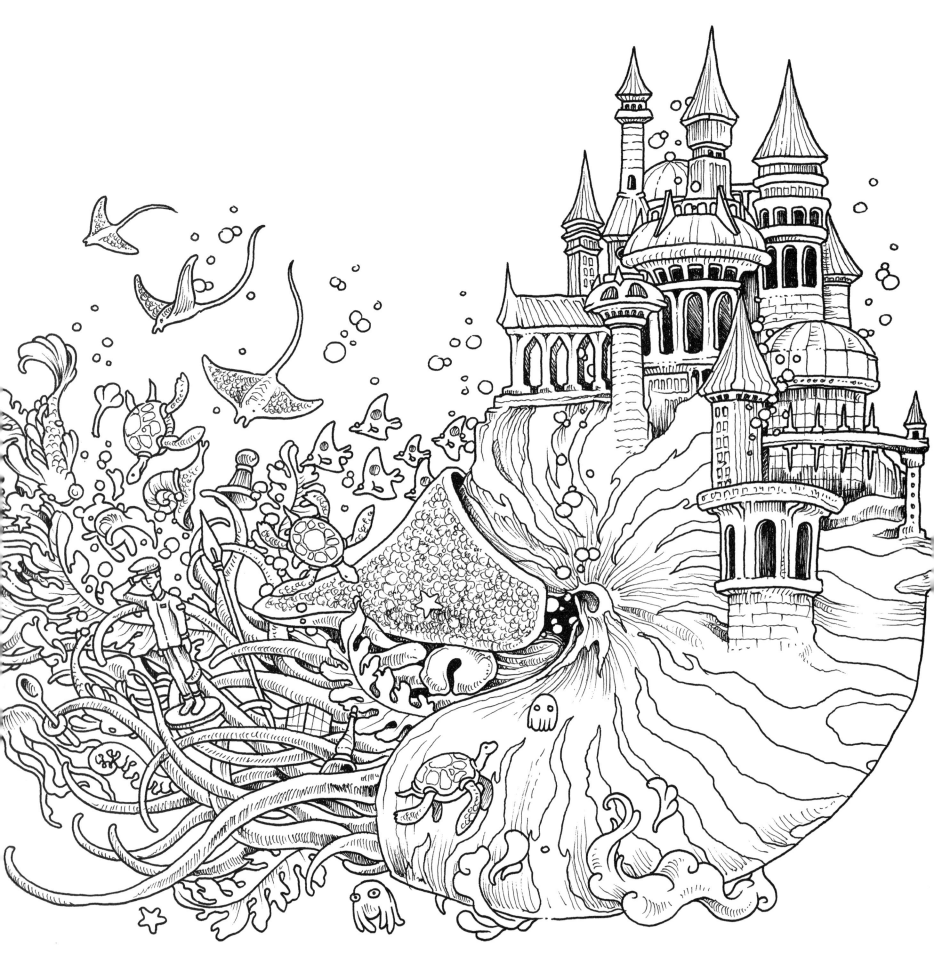

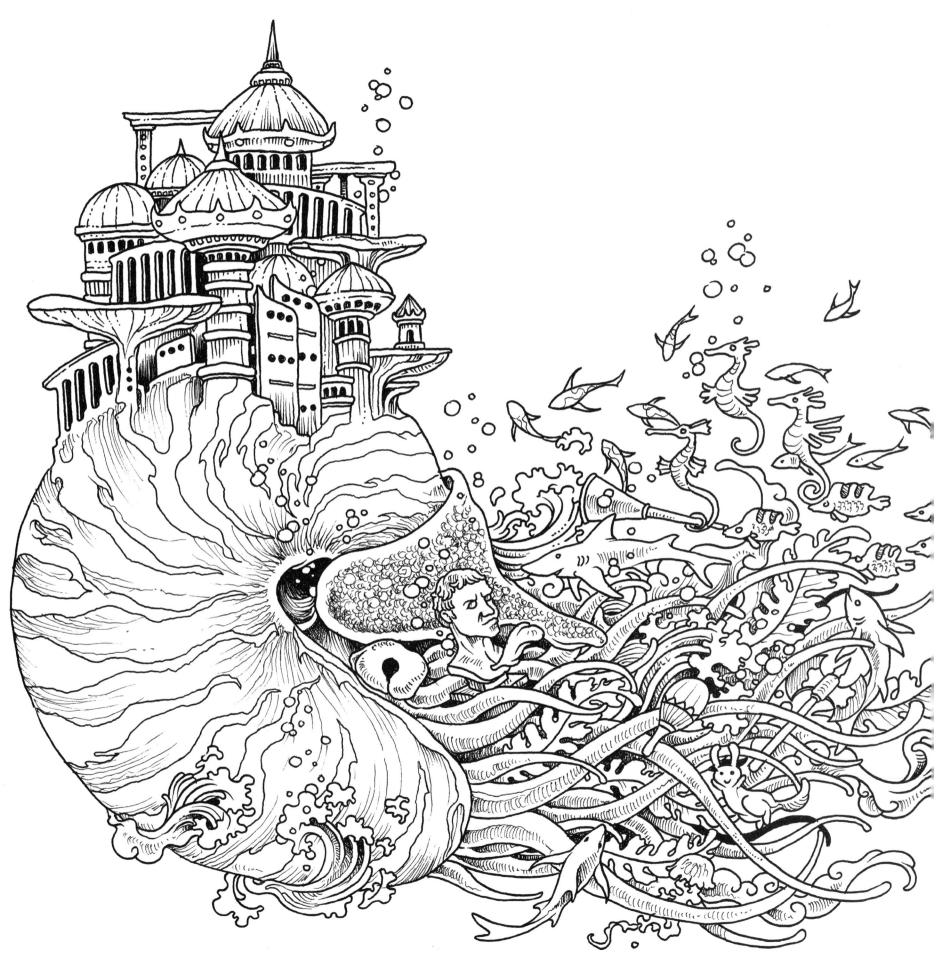

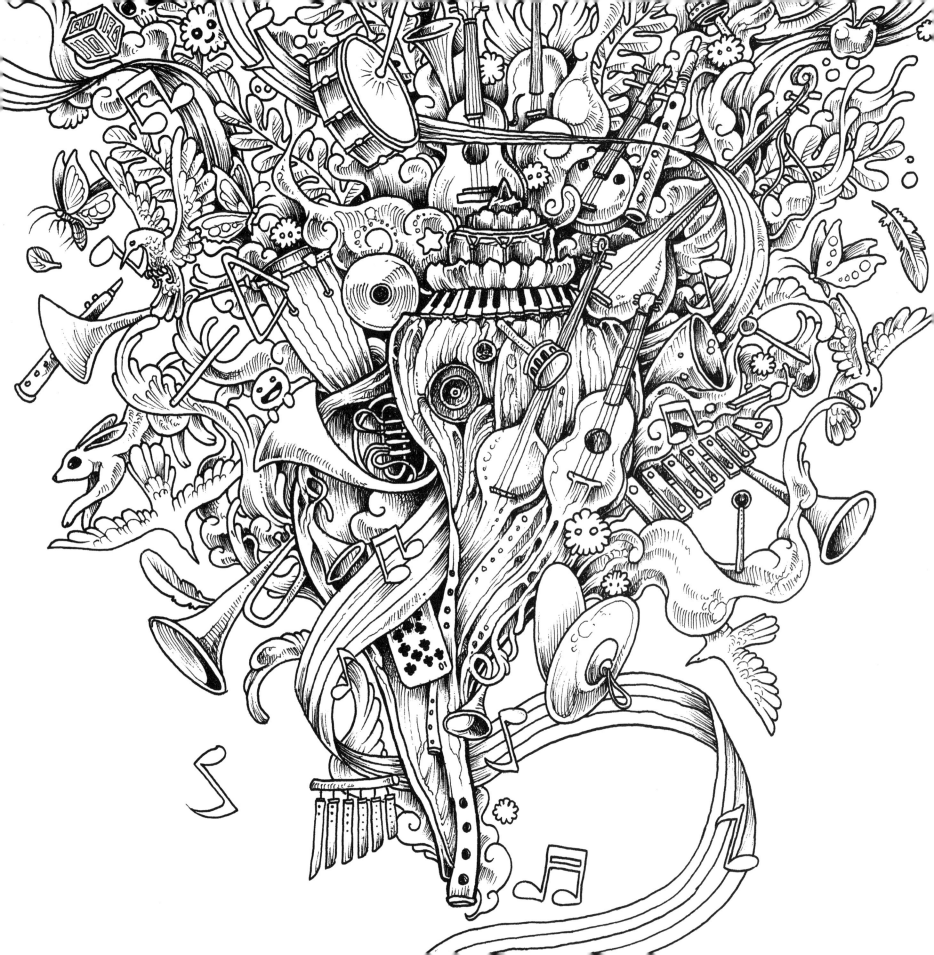

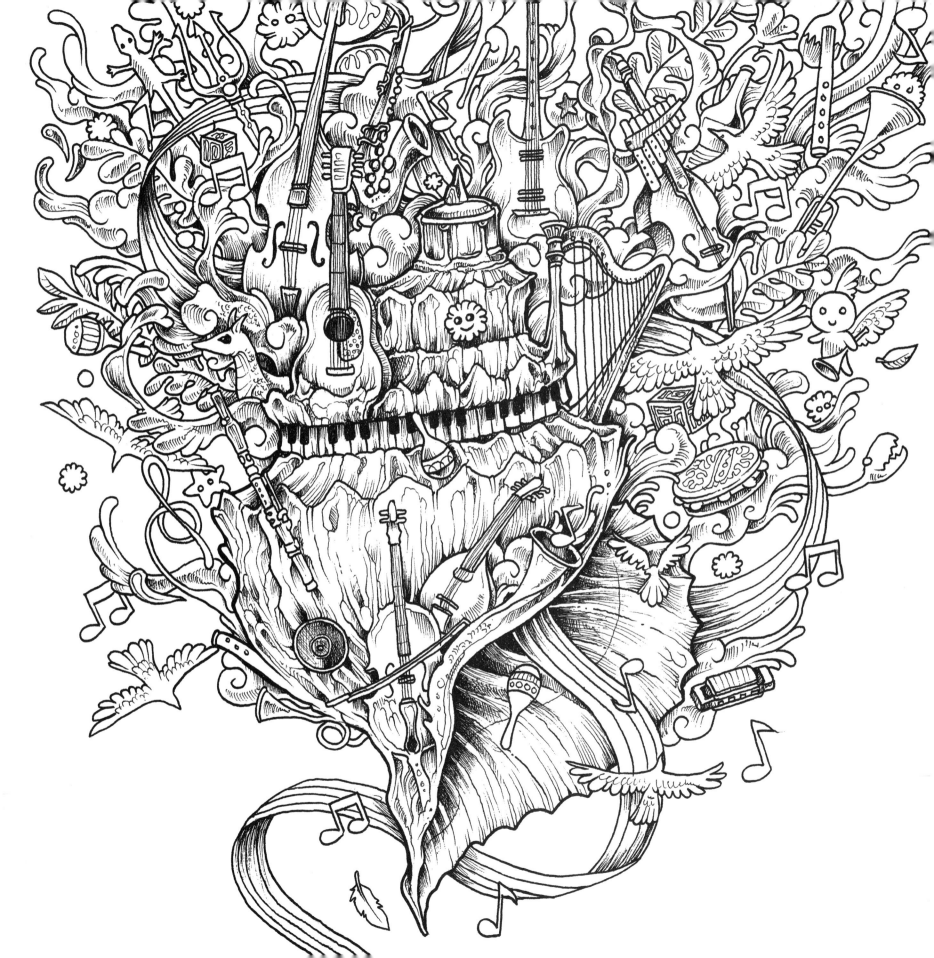

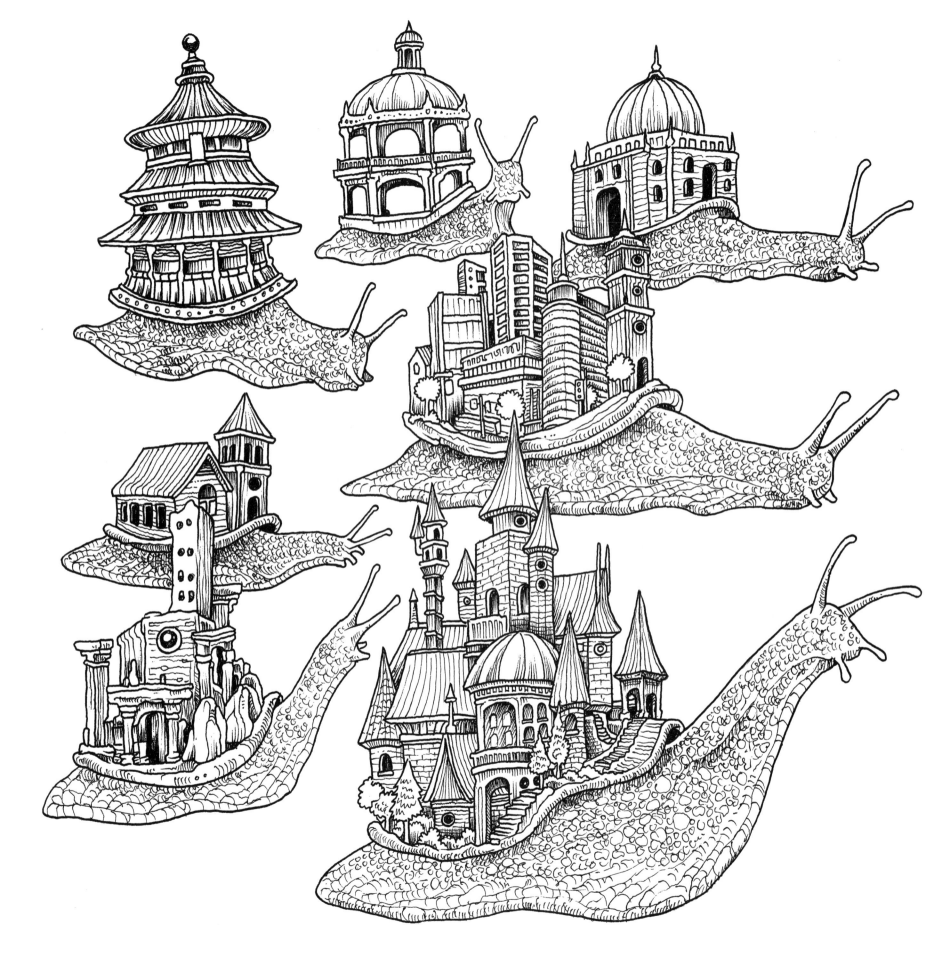

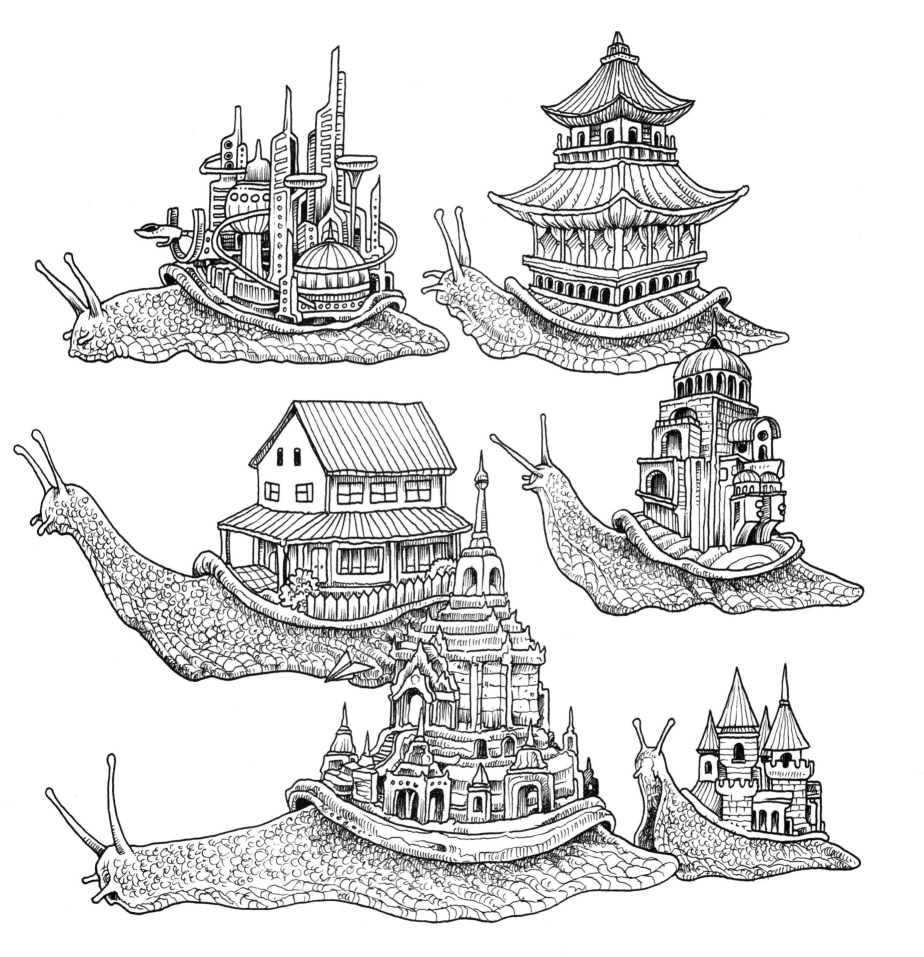

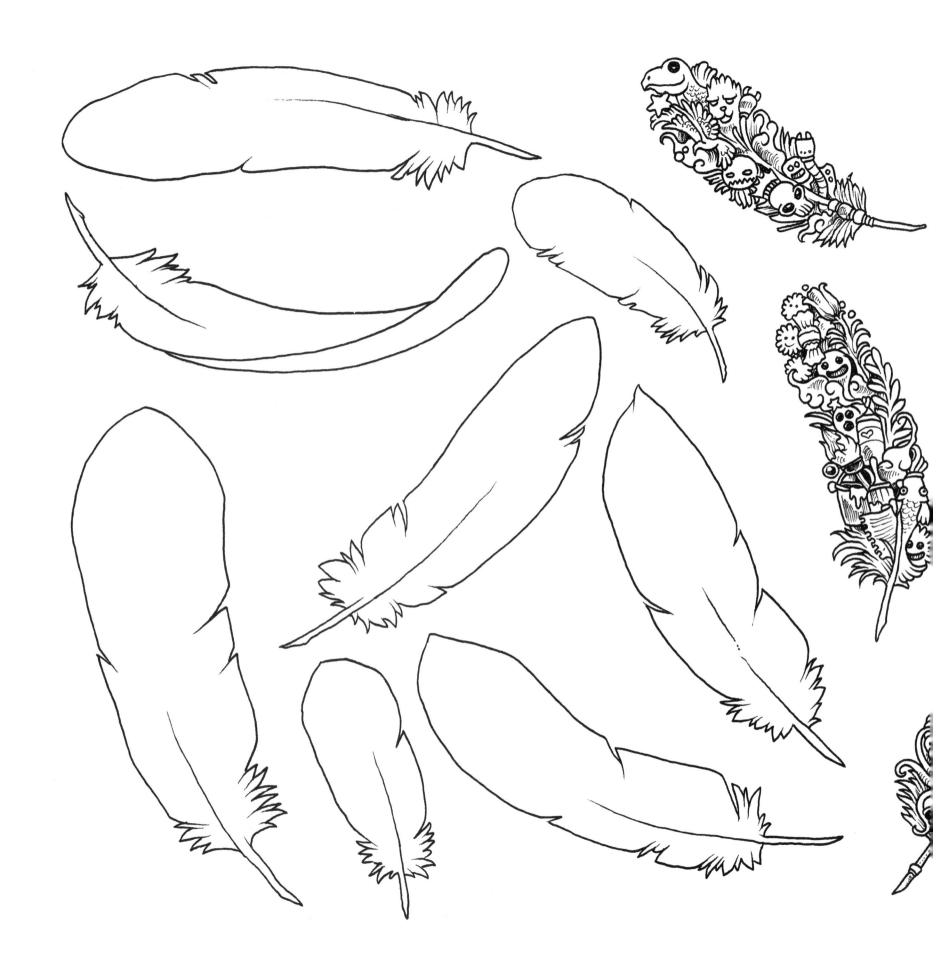

Complete the feathers.

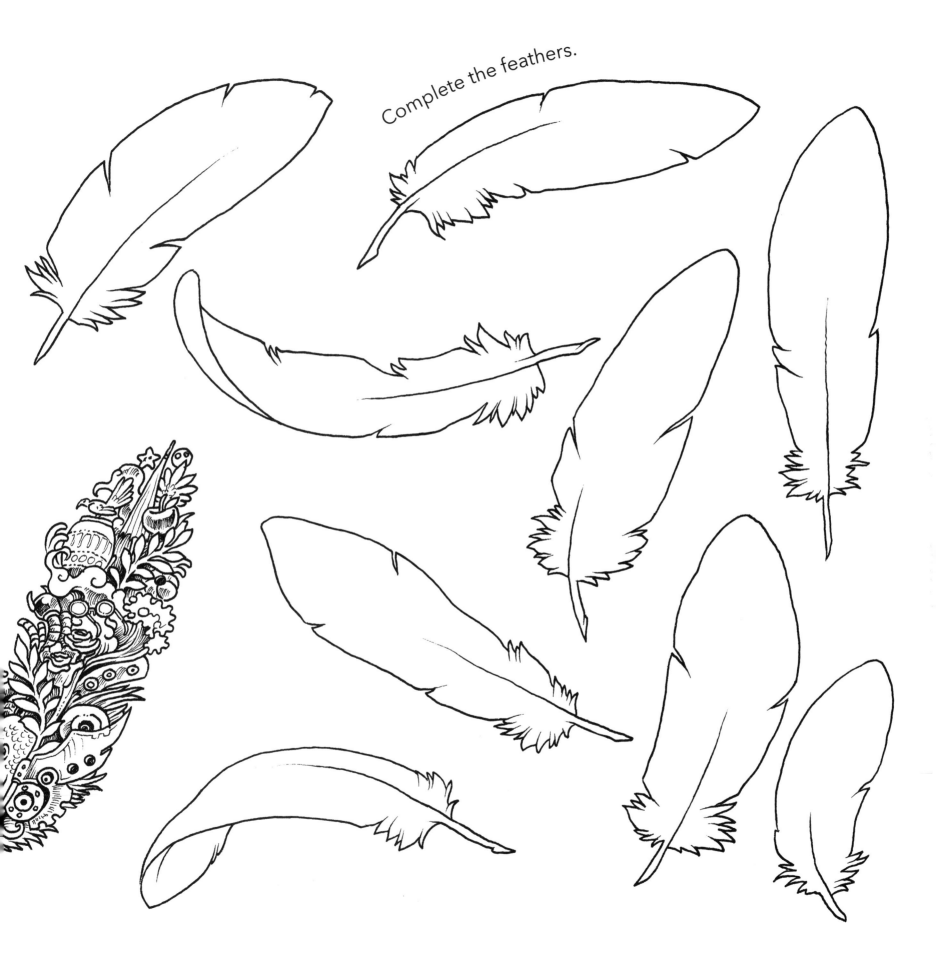

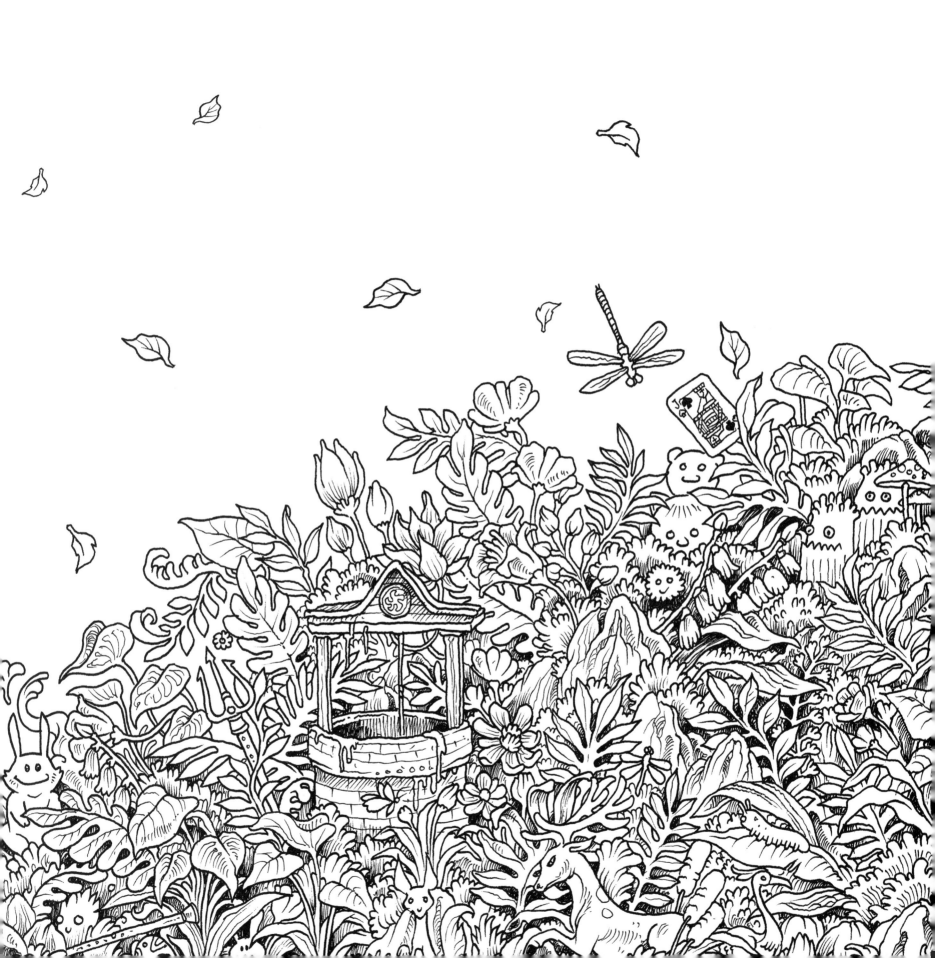

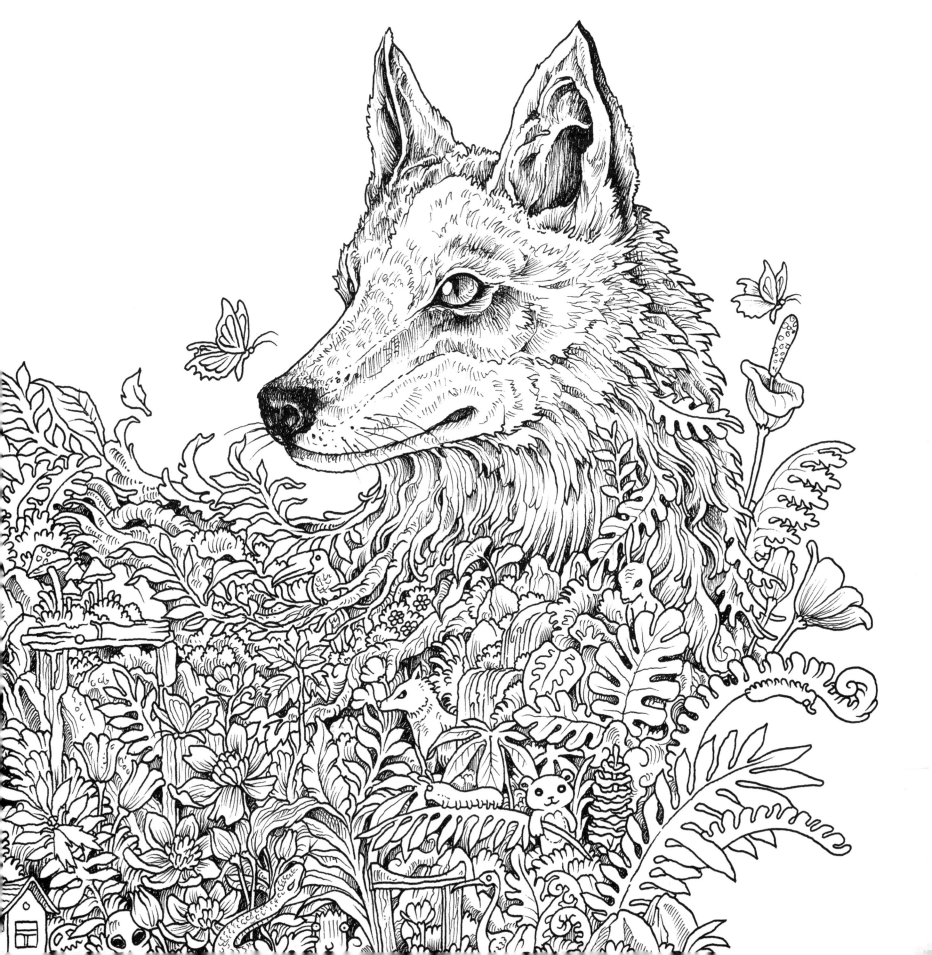

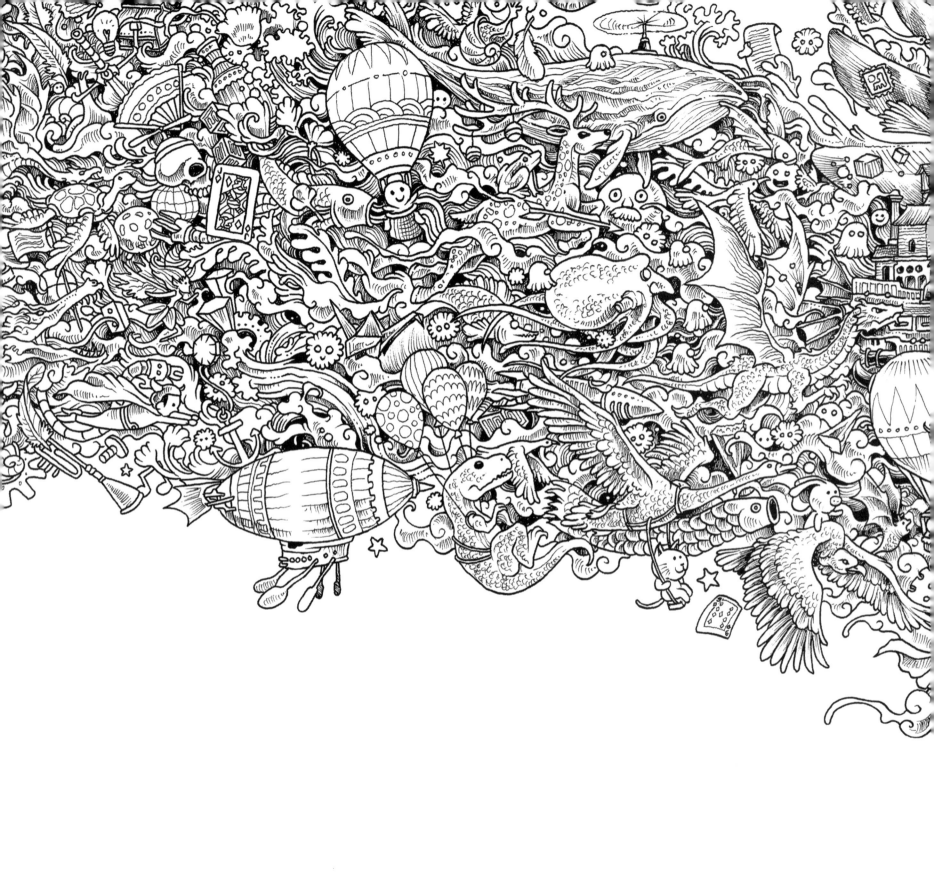

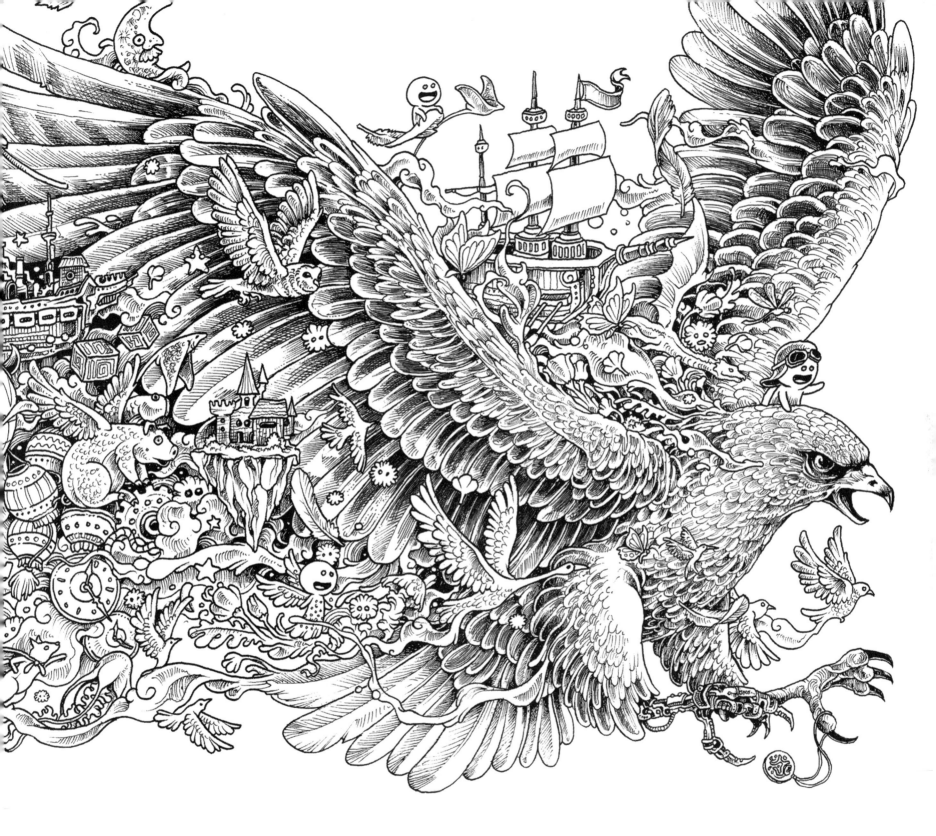

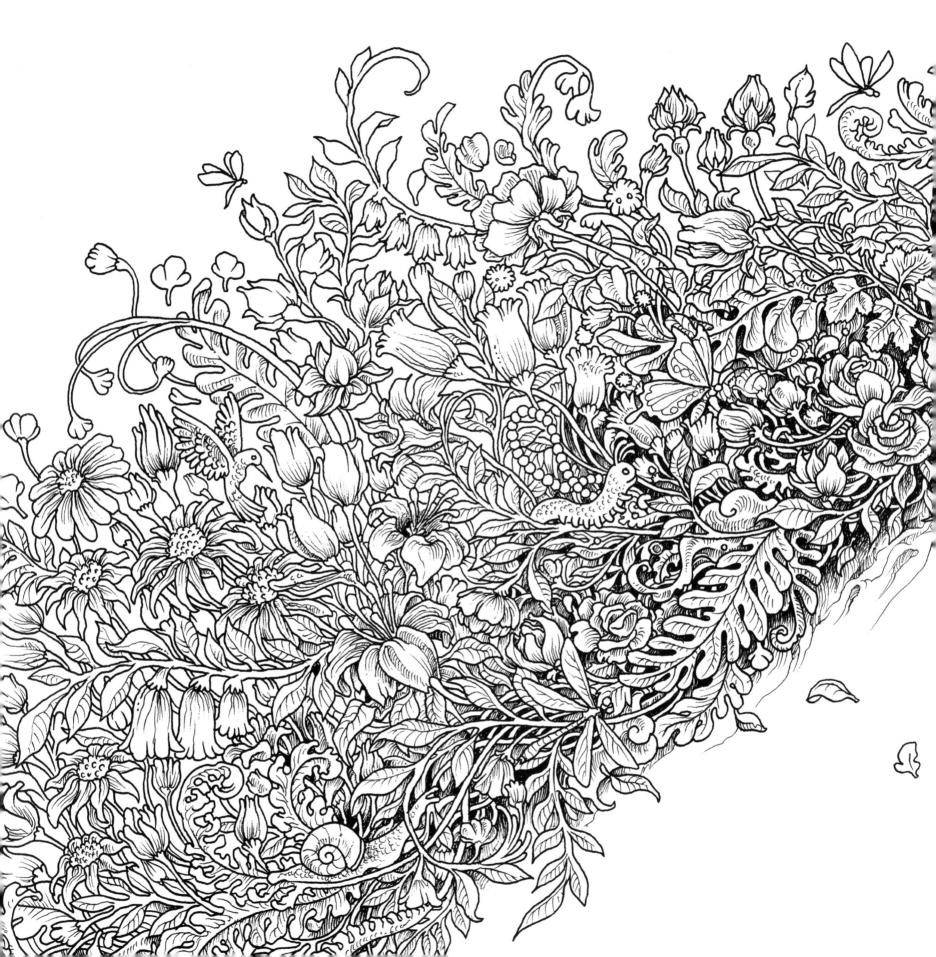

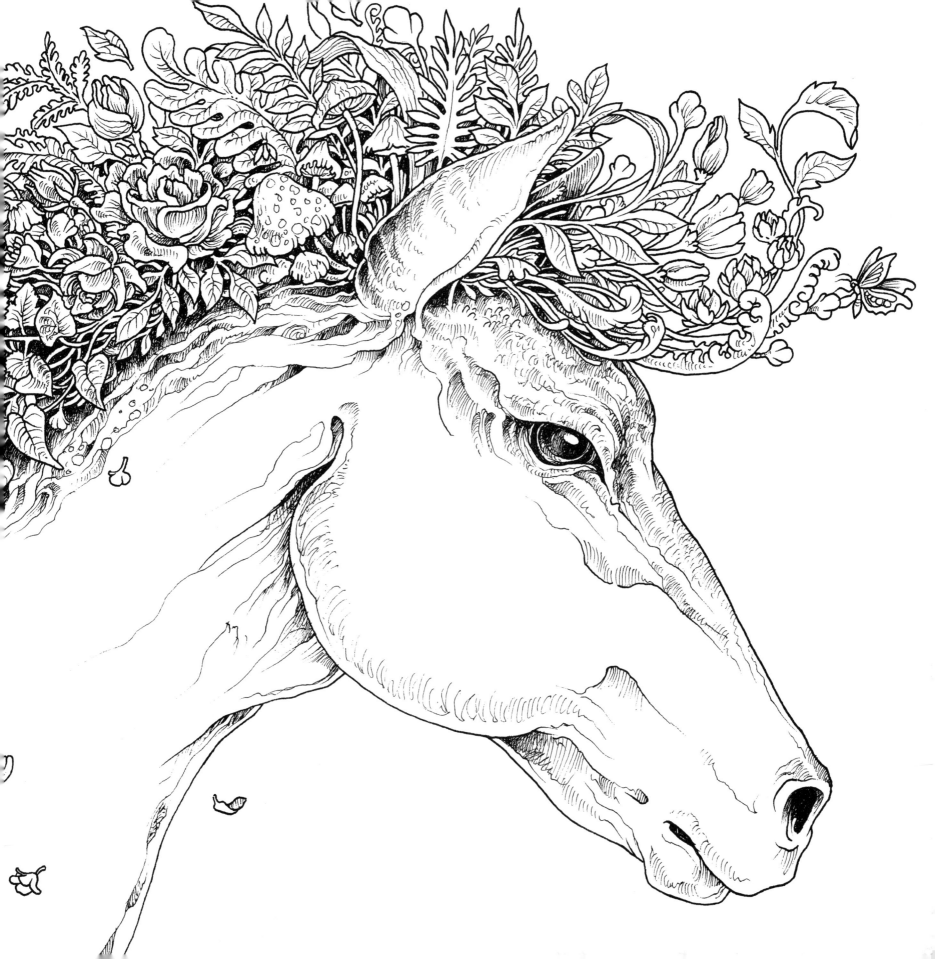

Can you find these items, artifacts, and creatures in the book?

When you have discovered them, color in the objects on the next few pages.

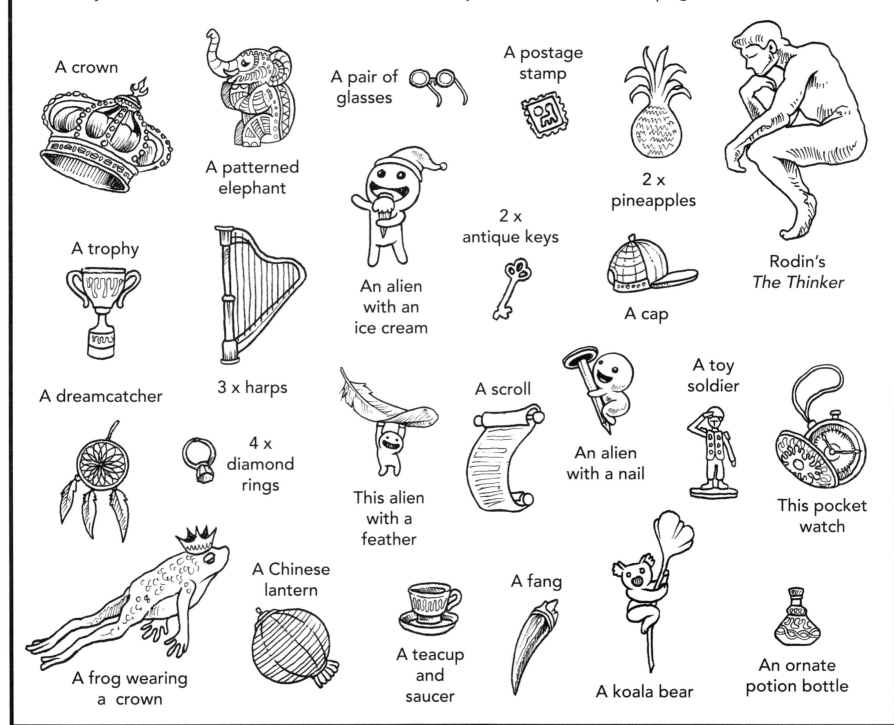

A crown

A patterned elephant

A pair of glasses

A postage stamp

2 x pineapples

A trophy

2 x antique keys

A cap

Rodin's *The Thinker*

An alien with an ice cream

A dreamcatcher

3 x harps

4 x diamond rings

This alien with a feather

A scroll

An alien with a nail

A toy soldier

This pocket watch

A frog wearing a crown

A Chinese lantern

A teacup and saucer

A fang

A koala bear

An ornate potion bottle

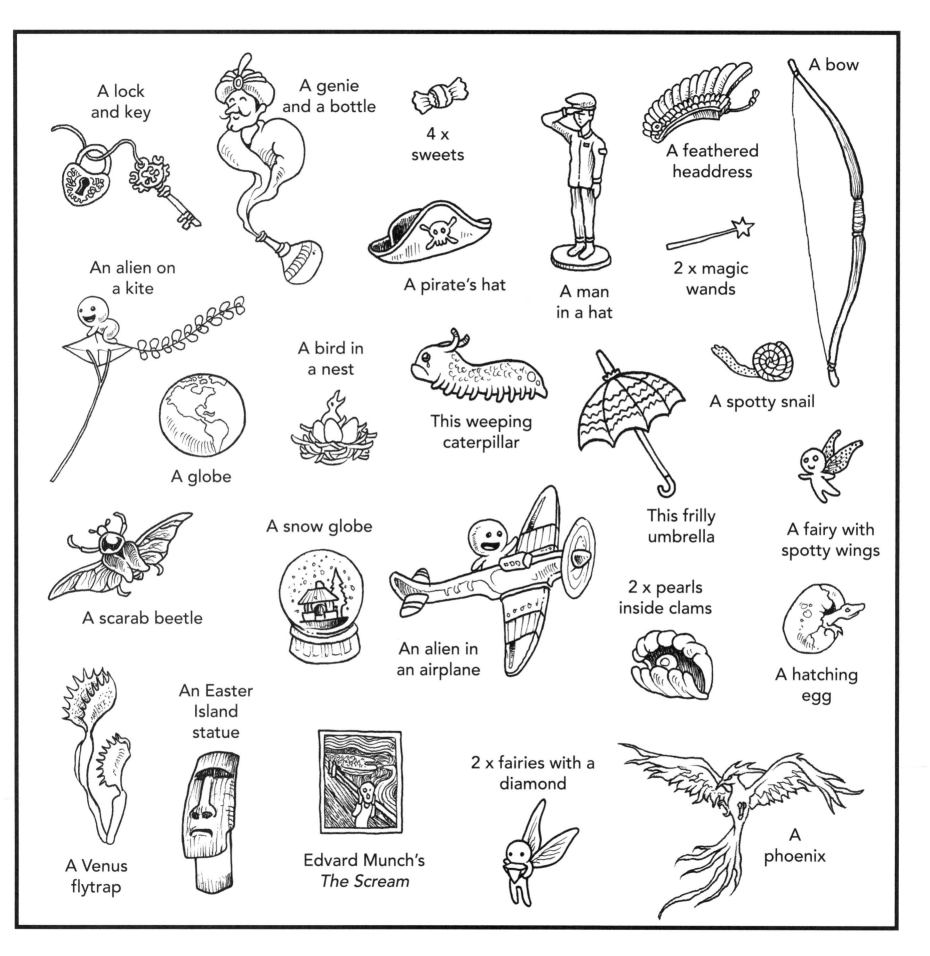

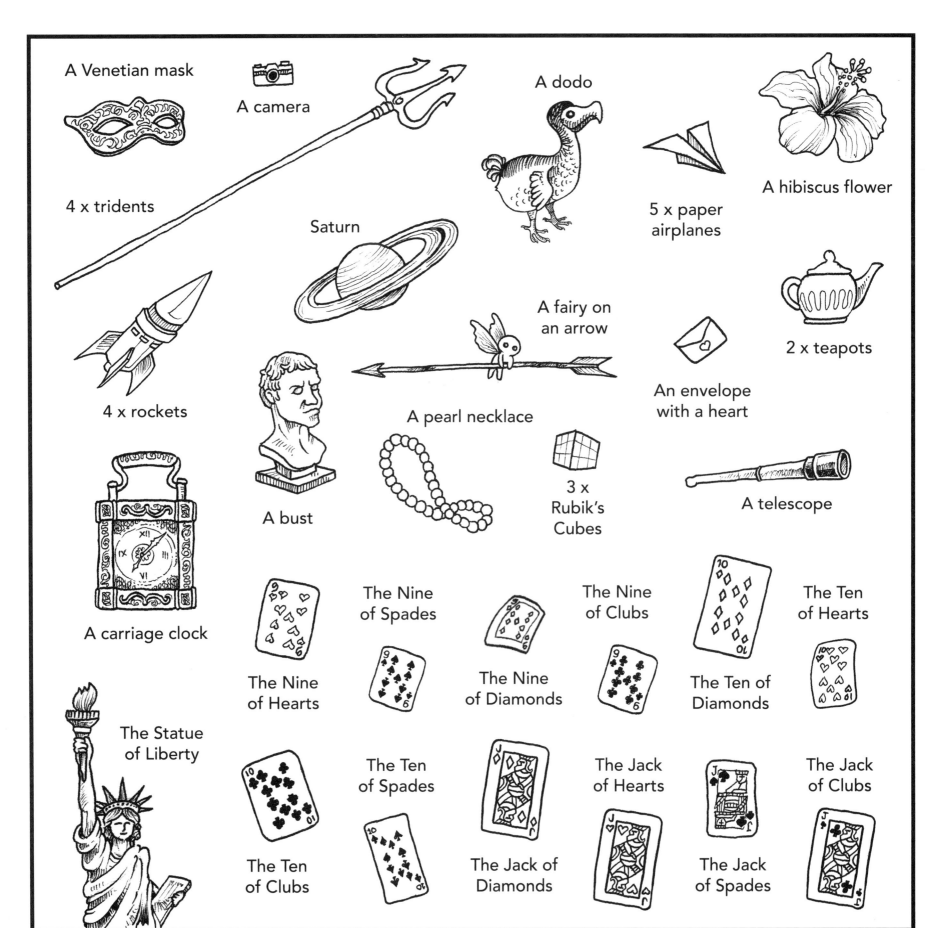

A Venetian mask

A camera

4 x tridents

A dodo

5 x paper airplanes

A hibiscus flower

Saturn

A fairy on an arrow

2 x teapots

4 x rockets

A bust

A pearl necklace

3 x Rubik's Cubes

An envelope with a heart

A telescope

A carriage clock

The Statue of Liberty

The Nine of Hearts

The Nine of Spades

The Nine of Diamonds

The Nine of Clubs

The Ten of Hearts

The Ten of Diamonds

The Ten of Clubs

The Ten of Spades

The Jack of Diamonds

The Jack of Hearts

The Jack of Spades

The Jack of Clubs

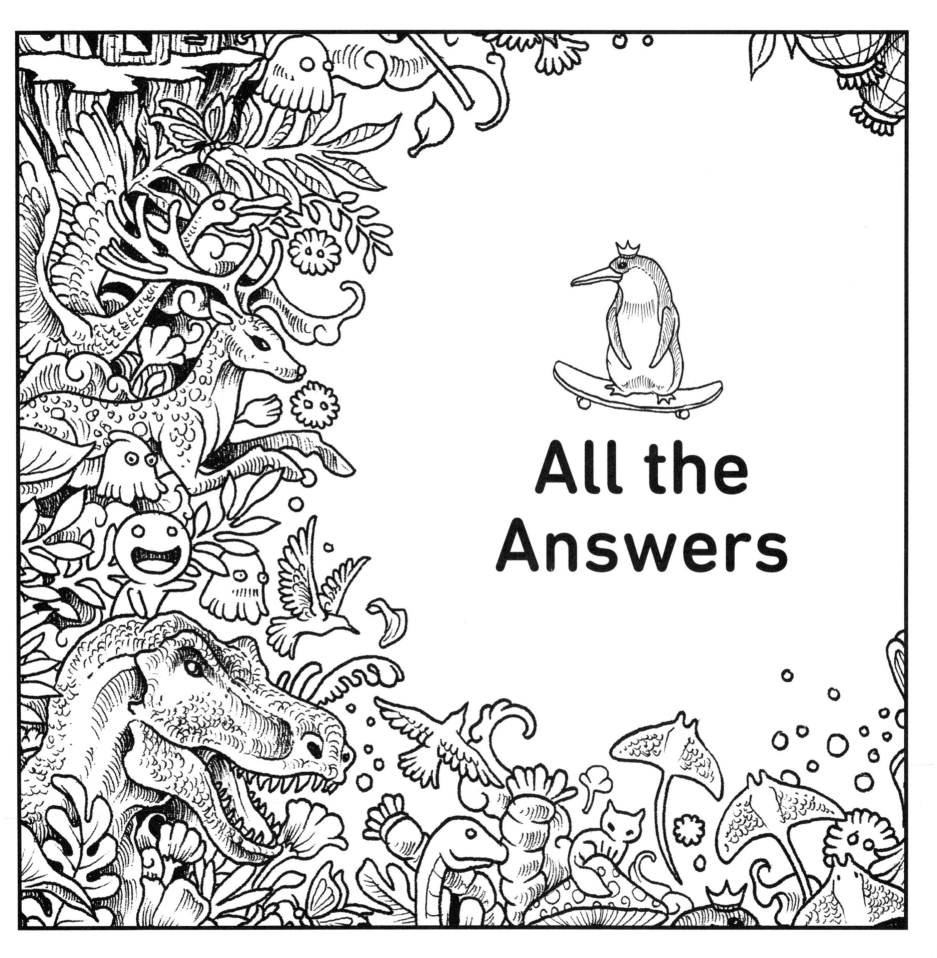

All the Answers

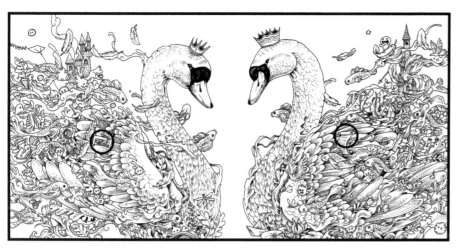

The Jack of Clubs and a scroll

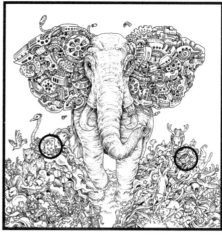

The Ten of Hearts and a Rubik's Cube

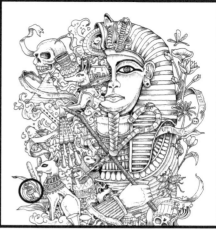

A toy soldier

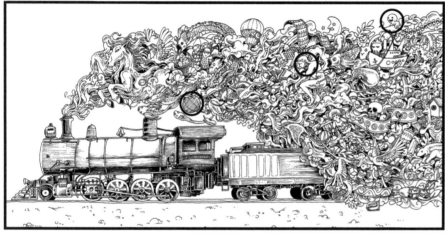

A Chinese lantern, Rodin's *The Thinker*, and an alien on a kite

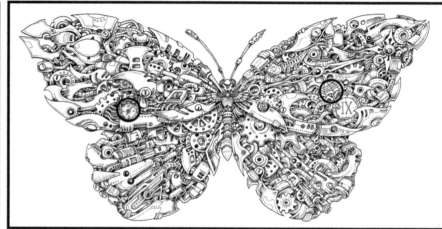

A carriage clock and a frilly umbrella

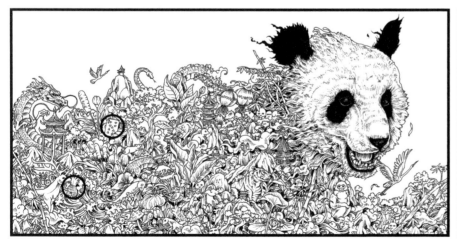

A pineapple and the Nine of Hearts

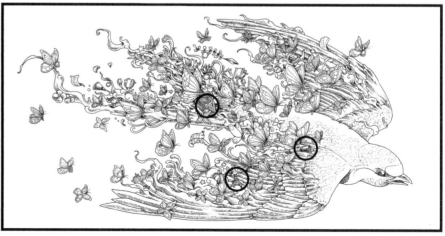

Edvard Munch's *The Scream*, an ornate potion bottle, and a telescope

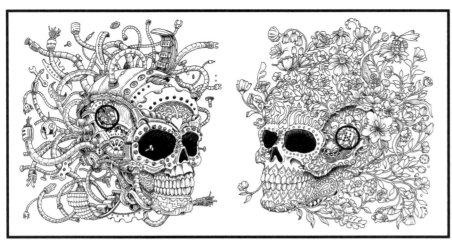

A pocket watch and the Nine of Clubs

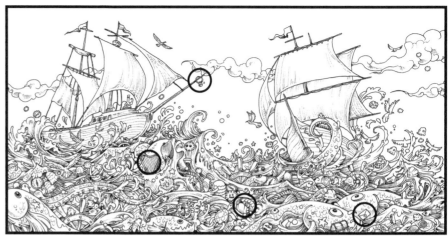

A harp, a diamond ring, a pearl inside a clam,
and an envelope with a heart on it

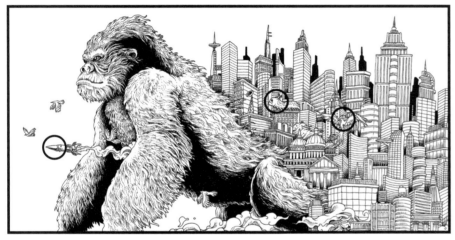

A rocket, a weeping caterpillar, and a phoenix

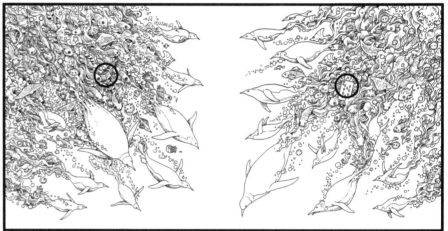

A Rubik's Cube and the Ten of Diamonds

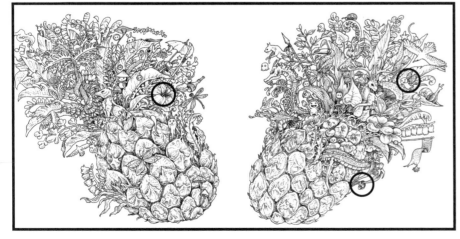

A hibiscus flower, a diamond ring, and
a fairy with spotty wings

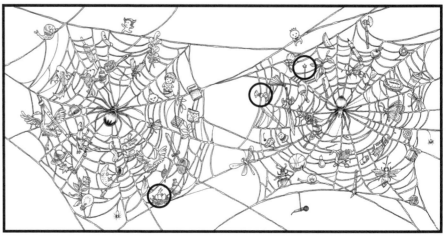

A bird in a nest, a sweet, and a magic wand

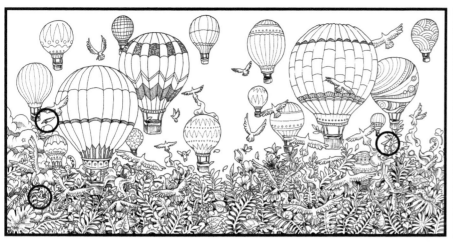

A koala bear and two paper airplanes

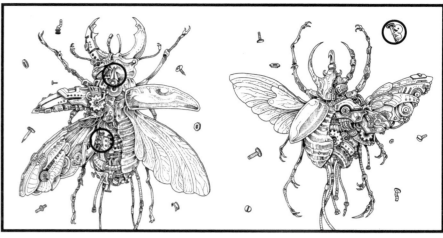

An antique key, a paper airplane, and an alien with a nail

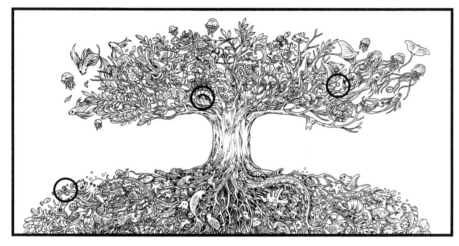

A diamond ring, a pearl inside a clam, and a magic wand

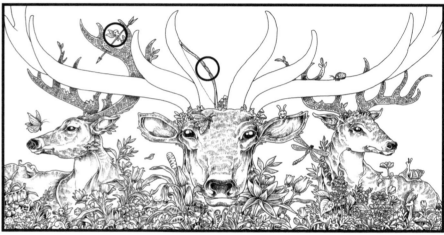

A fairy on an arrow and a bow

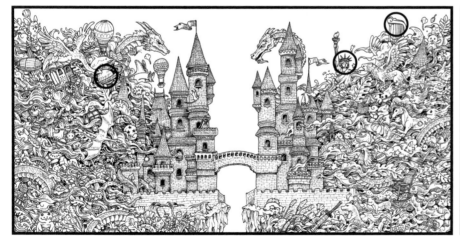

Saturn, the Statue of Liberty, and a harp

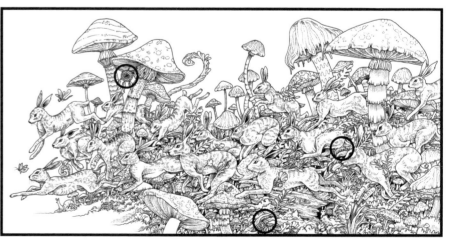

A dreamcatcher, a spotty snail, and a Venus flytrap